A TRANSPACIFIC POETICS

A TRANSPACIFIC POETICS

EDITED BY

LISA SAMUELS & SAWAKO NAKAYASU

LITMUS PRESS
BROOKLYN, 2017

ISBN: 978-1-933959-32-0

Cover art by Dagmar Vaikalafi Dyck
Front cover: *Seven sisters*, printed hahnemuehle paper with acrylic and indian ink, 2016
Back cover: *Fringe skirts*, acrylic and indian ink on builder's paper with pandanus
    and wool, 2016
Images courtesy of Gus Fisher Gallery, University of Auckland
Photo Credit: Sam Hartnell
Design and typesetting by HR Hegnauer

Litmus Press is a program of Ether Sea Projects, Inc., a 501(c)(3) non-profit
literature and arts organization. Dedicated to supporting innovative,
cross-genre writing, the press publishes the work of translators, poets, and
other writers, and organizes public events in their support. We encourage
interaction between poets and visual artists by featuring contemporary
artworks on the covers of our books. By actualizing the potential linguistic,
cultural, and political benefits of international literary exchange, we aim
to ensure that our poetic communities remain open-minded and vital.

State of the Arts

NYSCA

Litmus Press publications are made possible by the New York State Council on the
Arts with support from Governor Andrew Cuomo and the New York State Legislature.
Additional support for Litmus Press comes from the Leslie Scalapino – O Books
Fund, individual members and donors. All contributions are fully tax-deductible.

Cataloging-in-publication data is available from the Library of Congress.

Litmus Press
925 Bergen Street, Suite 405
Brooklyn, New York 11238
litmuspress.org

Small Press Distribution
1341 Seventh Street
Berkeley, California 94710
spdbooks.org

WHAT DO WE MEAN WHEN WE SAY TRANSPACIFIC

LISA SAMUELS

> The word "authentic" to me means that a person's not being manipulated nor alienated from their context or surrounding values, so authenticity can vary, and be peripatetic—in the sense of "authenticity" lending value to a place, a person, an object and so on.[1]
>
> —Pam Brown

> But it is impossible to make use of the sea.[2]
>
> —Édouard Glissant

When you live in Oceania, you see the word "Transpacific" on freight company trucks, waste containers, and trade deals. The word seems to know where the interaction is: deliverables among end points. Another aspect of the word transpacific emphasizes the transitive itself, or simply *trans*, with internal difference where transitions are. That difference obtains within and among people who move their goods, places that receive and tend and send out, language that extends and bends back meanings: all of these absorb and diffract exponential internal difference. In other words, transpacific labels a concept that extends from commodification to geography to identity flow and beyond. Useful books like Martin Edmond's *Fenua Imi: the Pacific in History and Imagination* (2002) consider how long centuries of contact and post-contact—of Occident with Oceania—proliferate ideas and thick memory about what we mean when we say transpacific.

As Epeli Hauʻofa's resonant essay "Our Sea of Islands" (1993) indicates, a major part of Oceania's cultural concepts is that the ocean is a positive *place*, not, or not only, a transit zone. The ocean's surfaces and depths have cultural location and consequence, maps and identities, visibility as well as invisibility. We often look at rivers as having identity and defining their places: the Waikato, the Han, the Hudson, the Murray, the Cagayan. Meanwhile the ocean, vast and replete with

---

1 Pam Brown, "Authentic Local: an illustrated autobiographical sample of an itinerant local's pursuits in poetry & art," *Ka Mate Ka Ora* 13 (2014): 39–40.
2 Édouard Glissant, *L'Intention poétique* (Paris: Éditions du Seuil, 1969): 247. My translation. The original reads: "Mais il est impossible de se servir de la mer."

flora and fauna and topography, mostly impenetrable to the natural eye, challenges our ability to see it as place, with the same right to meaning and being normatively accorded to rivers and to land. Doubtless the difficulty of harnessing its forces, as Édouard Glissant knows, is part of this history of our unseeing.

Learning the rights and being of the ocean is both tactile and conceptual, both ecological and ontological. The tactility of its dispersed being exceeds us: the ocean is so large we cannot know or remember it, we cannot keep it all in mind. In this way the ocean is one example of the challenge of perceiving what exceeds single identity, what is not one thing. Since everything and everyone exceeds single identity, the ocean is the largest being on this planet that questions our ability to perceive being. As a being, the ocean constitutes the paradox of the unencompassable. It suggests our need for compassionate attention to the lineaments of our perceptual abilities and concomitantly toward the beings of others, all those that cannot be singly identified as they go about their right to be. The ocean represents in macrocosm what the rights are of any being.

Thinking in ecological terms that the ocean is one unencompassable being inter-swirling makes Oceania perceivable as an exemplar and embodiment of the globalization of cultural imaginaries. Just as there is no center of the ocean, there is no center of the surface of the world. In response to value shifts that recognize these conditions, some people consider everyone to be marginal now. Rather than embracing shared marginality, I prefer to imagine the importance of each being in terms of "distributed centrality." This shift in emphasis is a consequence of seeing the globalized world as equal in its rights and the value of its bodies. Taking its cue from "distributed cognition," distributed centrality insists on the equal import of every place, person, and event as the center of its doings. Logically, saying we are all marginal and saying we are all central is arguably the same thing. Politically, however, distributed centrality names an ethical emphasis. Everywhere and everyone is the center of attention.

Such metaphors bring us back to a problem of contact: in a wet "butterfly effect," we can put our hand in the ocean anywhere and be in touch with ocean everywhere. But when you are *here*, a deictic that shifts wherever you are, the definitions of culture are not so penetrable, and they often flinch in response to what's perceived as outside touch. We can feel these differentials in matters such as intellectual property (see Barry Barclay's keen points about public domain in *Mana Tuturu*, 2005[3]) and

---

3 Barry Barclay, *Mana Tuturu: Māori Treasures and Intellectual Property Rights* (Auckland: Auckland University Press, 2005): see for example 186–198 on Māori tikanga, or "customary law."

access in the digitas. The dangerous pleasure of imagining the digitas to be oceanic—you put your hand in to the Internet anywhere you touch one of its devices—makes the contemporary moment of considering the transpacific mimetically keen.

By the digitas, I mean digital performativity with constitutive perfusing by the techne and humans involved. We interact with Internet protocols, and we make and are made by the consequent webs, with our habitus, the civitas, and the digits of our fingers. As our identities perfuse into cross-national and cross-linguistic imaginaries, it's useful to consider what happens when an English-dominant zone, the Internet, is imagined at the same moments as multi-lingual and multi-local, multi-*here*, imaginaries. What happens to non-urban vitalities in a digitas that skews urban: bundled group acts with expectations of outside views that enlarge hits and transactions? Given the code-level English-dominance of the Internet, what happens when a book like this is presented in and as Englishes? How do we recognize the distributed centrality of the translingual? What versions of "trans" apply, and who gets to say?

These and other considerations helped me, and my co-editor Sawako Nakayasu, think about what a transpacific poetics might look like. In this collection, one among many imaginable versions of regional poetics, transpacific is between waters and permeating waters; it's a concept that sometimes flies "over" the Pacific and sometimes hovers intra-Pacific, among islands, and that is always between places in or on the edge of the Pacific Ocean. Chile and Australia, Japan and Aotearoa/New Zealand, the United States and Korea. Moving our friendship into making something of our conversations about what we mean when we say transpacific, Sawako and I sought out writings that crossed borders and inhabited boundaries involving at least two zones of sustained Pacific living. The resulting crossings also crucially include both northern and southern hemispheres.

The keenest focus of this collection is contemporary transcultural experimental poetries and poetics that witness Pacific consequences. We want *more* works that are affectively committed to intra-Oceania, transpacific, cross-hemispheric poetic thinking. Although it is a "gathering of flowers," to invoke the Greek etymology, this book is not bidding to anthologize in the exclusionary sense. We hope the inclusions and lacunae here will lead to other new collections with their own experimental oceanic transculturalisms. In an era when globalization does not seem to have shaken off single-origin defaults—in other words, in an era when so many people still assume everyone has *a* nationality and a single place where they are *from*, when so many literary collections continue to be organized according to sole-nation origin—this collection works to bolster a poetics of transitivity and transnationalism.

We started this work because we believe in the artistic and ethical visions of such transculturalisms. Our own lives are shaped by mixings of cultures, languages, and artistic traditions and modes. In addition to time spent in China, Sawako lives between the United States and Japan; I've lived in different parts of the U.S., in Europe, in the Middle East, in Malaysia, and since 2006 in Aotearoa/New Zealand. The critical work of Susan Schultz and others bears witness to the trickiness of being transplanted (for Schultz, to Hawai'i) and remaining, from some points of view, perpetually in the sensitized newcomer position. For most of the writers in this book, varieties of the transpacific are regular cultural context(s), home(s), and/or origin(s).

Imagining a transpacific poetics includes imagining a right to participate in its articulation. The concepts "right to speak" and "right to be" are now generally accorded to peoples who have been in an identity or place for as long as we can remember. Thus indigenous and eco-critical studies honor first peoples and first places with a right to speak and perform their being. Inhabiting a blended speaking in relation to historical actions summed up in the word colonialism, the Pacific and many other parts of the world live in a discomfited cultural imaginary that can be thought of as "settlementopia." As with distributed centrality, the process of making *A TransPacific Poetics* prompted me to conceive this new portmanteau term combining "settlement" and "_topia." The blank before "topia" indicates its ambivalence: _topia is neither dystopia nor utopia, but a constative and an incompletion that is a call to action. I mean settlementopia to be involved with ideas and experiences of settlement and what you do with it now and, again, who gets to say. Colonial myths of Oceania utopias meet the dystopic dangers of doing nothing, saying nothing, as cultures constitute and reconstitute. In present-day shifts to globalization and the digitas, settlementopia is located within continuing places and actions and within live bodies themselves, within contests about linguistic and national and personal identity. Many texts in this collection signify, like Craig Santos Perez's "fatal impact statements," such impacted bodies.

Some people might say that settlement is obsolete and we are all post-colonial now. Settlementopia is another word for the problematic dream that we can be post-history. It responds to Stephen Turner's theory of colonial forgetting, in which "putting the past behind us," treating history as past rather than present, masks ongoing conditions. For Turner, "postcolonial" is a misnomer, a global not-yet.[4] One can consider settlementopia within "time's cycle" as potentially contested recurrences of forms, seasons, ceremonies, and cultural values. Not everything cultural must change, in such cycles. One can also consider settlementopia within

---

4   Stephen Turner, "Settler Dreaming," *Memory Connection Journal* 1.1 (December 2011): 114–17. Turner also addresses "colonial forgetting" in other writings.

"time's arrow," as contemporary poetry and poetics, performed and expository, does its work amidst loud global "progress" rhetorics of managerialism and efficiency. The _topia of our contexts, trying to figure out how to constitute and imagine this moment's globalizing cultures, has the Janus-faced pull of past-ward and future-ward strengths. Which one is "good" for what cultural value? When one reads Barbara Jane Reyes's untranslated Baybayin script, *when* is the position of reading? Does history get disgorged into the present; does the present invert itself like a sea cucumber towards a revivified positive anachronism?[5]

In addition to helping think the transpacific, settlementopia can be relevant to thinking one's position in other parts of the world that have been *visited upon* over the last millennia. The condition of being transited is multiple—moving actively outward from a place, displacing others from a place and/or being displaced, linking one place to another place, becoming aware of one's links with transiting peoples, linking one or more set of peoples-in-place with other sets of peoples-in-place—and settlementopia describes one of many conditions that interact in re-shaped lands, cross-cultural transits, transnational identities, efforts at recovering and protecting the indigenous, efforts to "re-home" refugees, and cultural events and technical forces within the digitas. In all of this, settlementopia designates what it cannot finally circumscribe, and its nullity is absolute in the legal sense: the consequences of its infixed blank ("_") potentially concern anyone. That blank can be seen as a feature of imagination's power to gain by making room for response, not by yielding but by changing the terms of assertion and creation. I think of Eileen Tabios inviting the Filipino expression "hay naku" into poetic form, making room for its constative "oh" in a form that is a willed cousin of the haiku.

If settlementopia can help consider such contested issues, its status understood as unresolvable, then the term transhuman might be preferred for the identities we negotiate. Currently, the term "post-human" questions the reduction of identity configuration to the lineaments of one particular humanoid biomass, as well as drawing attention to the bodily implications of distributed cognition. The trouble I have with "post-human" is that it renders past or obsolete, at a lexical level, the very person that human polity and theory need always to consider. The term transhuman might more strongly emphasize the interfacing body. It isn't "post" or *over*; it connects. As Corey Wakeling proposes, a fertile poetic ecology

---

5 Kolokesa Māhina-Tuai writes about "a Moana/Pacific belief that we walk forward into the past and backward into the future, both of which are constantly mediated in the changing present, where the past is put in front as a guiding principle and the future, situated behind, is brought to bear on past experiences" (*South* 2 [2013], 13); quoted in Lisa Samuels, *Over Hear: six types of poetry experiment in Aotearoa/New Zealand* (Tinfish, 2015), 13.

is precisely consanguineous with our connection to earthy ecology. Moreover, the term transhuman indexes the participatory centrality of the trans body: as with Jai Arun Ravine's expressed feeling of being a "man joiner," as with their film *TOM / TRANS / THAI*, as with the importance of personal pronouns that recognize the right of LGBTQI self-naming, the transhuman helps to hold open what it means to be human.

The work in this book exemplifies forces we can access by writing rings around the conditions of settlementopia and related transpacific imaginaries. Those rings can be black holes, as in Don Mee Choi's description of Kim Hyesoon's poetry: "Princess Abandoned's hell is a *black mirror*. Kim's hell extends from this black mirror, remaining counter-patriarchal, possessing nothing, reflecting and resisting *Mr. Military Officers with black ink*." Those rings can be shiny as they strike through resistance: Murray Edmond takes us through his childhood to the bodily "trans" liberation of *The Rocky Horror Show*, conceived in the settlementopia of semi-rural Aotearoa/New Zealand and become a devotional cinematic text, *The Rocky Horror Picture Show*, across the Pacific Ocean in the U.S.

Similar contra-mapping and cross-placement is recorded in many other pieces in *A TransPacific Poetics*. Staggered typeface, drifting page area, text-holes, torn and resituated genre conventions: these are modes of simultaneously discomfited and empowered re-mapping. The translingual blends in Sean Labrador y Manzano's words—"beneath oilskin subduct palay moonless stirrups measure syncope"—and jams to overlaps that perform the challenge of perception in the typeface measures of Lehua M. Taitano. If the ocean were surveyed with floating monument studs like those used in land surveys, the monuments would sink and rise, always on the move, an image akin to Stuart Cooke's conception of location as "open system." When I came to Oceania I thought about the oceanic as mobile interstices akin to neurological dendritic gaps, wet electric areas whose contact is somatically virtual, whose material discontinuities are what permit attention's speed. That transaction compares to touch, whose infusions are theoretically even more dimensional than finger surfaces show, as "membranism" wants to say.[6] Seeing tracts of oceans that way—comparable to thinking-material, currents of energy with movement—can link with culturally-specific mappings of ocean and the skeins of star maps. To understand the ocean, Hauʻofa's "our sea of islands," as always both cultural *and* natural is to be in a constant state of mixing.

---

6 See Lisa Samuels, "Membranism, wet gaps, archipelago poetics" in *Reading Room: A Journal of Art and Culture* 4 (2010): 156–67. In other words, distributed centrality and settlementopia are always scored in the body of the person and the body of art.

Ocean's movement is a different kind of transplace that helps us understand what it means to be in place; mapping does not need to mimic the possession-maps of real-estated land. As Melanie Rands tells it, in white words on a black stellar page-mirror, "The map is not the territory." This kind of transpacific poetics re-imagines the relations between cultural politics and geophysics. The very name Aotearoa ("Land of the Long White Cloud," the Māori name for New Zealand), for example, describes the land by gesturing to what it is not—to the clouds nearby, outward and visible signs of the land's adjacent gaps. Such layering names a cultural geography that many of the works here also value as they layer ink and voice, languages and time, persons and soil and water, echoing Myung Mi Kim's urge to "call into question, to disclose, to make common" our conditions.

As with the title of this essay, "What do we mean when we say transpacific," leaving off the normative terminal punctuation underscores coexistent states of question and assertion in the thinking modes of this book. The deliberate retention of Commonwealth styles of spelling and punctuation in some of the pieces here also means to perform difference, to encourage the co-existence of alternative norms and expectations. I hope for ever more differential inter- and intra-oceanic experimental poetry and poetics—and, for that matter, for biopoetries involving words with seawater and diatoms. Would the future-ward techne of such biopoetries encroach on a literal oceanic right to be? How can such works be showcased while we wait for our electrified digitas to grow entirely liquid-tolerant? Could some works in this book move into bodily digitality or linguistic motion-capture? Well, that's partly a rhetorical question and a matter of how to perform such transformations, since many materials here can also be rendered digitally, such as Ya-Wen Ho's relentlessly over-inked identity piece. Such motion potential, for now, is performed by the act of your holding this book to read, for which I thank the contributing writers, my co-editor Sawako Nakayasu, the editors and designers of Litmus Press, and you.

> May 2014, Tāmaki Makaurau/Auckland, Aotearoa/New Zealand;
> June 2016, Seattle, U.S.

BIBLIOGRAPHY

Barclay, Barry. *Mana Tuturu: Māori Treasures and Intellectual Property Rights*. Auckland: Auckland University Press, 2005.

Brown, Pam. "Authentic Local: an illustrated autobiographical sample of an itinerant local's pursuits in poetry & art." *Ka Mate Ka Ora* 13 (2014): 1–45.

Edmond, Martin. *Fenua Imi: the Pacific in History and Imagination*. Christchurch: Bumper Books, 2002.

Glissant, Édouard. *L'Intention poétique*. Paris: Éditions du Seuil, 1969.

Hauʻofa, Epeli. "Our Sea of Islands." *The Contemporary Pacific* 6.1, Spring 1994, 147–61. First published in *A New Oceania: Rediscovering Our Sea of Islands*, edited by Vijay Naidu, Eric Waddell, and Epeli Hauʻofa. Suva: School of Social and Economic Development, The University of the South Pacific, 1993.

Samuels, Lisa. *Over Hear: six types of poetry experiment in Aotearoa/New Zealand*. Kāneʻohe: Tinfish Press, 2015.

--. "Membranism, wet gaps, archipelago poetics." *Reading Room: A Journal of Art and Culture* 4 (2010): 156–67.

Turner, Stephen. "Settler Dreaming." *Memory Connection Journal* 1.1 (December 2011): 114–126.

FREELY FRAYED

DON MEE CHOI

지금 막 도착한 핑크박스, 뚜껑이 열리길 기다리는 핑크박스, 이것을 껴안아보면 멀리서 온 것의 냄새가나. 그러나 한번 몸을 들여놓으면 그 누구도 여기를 나가지는 못해. 아아 귀여운 핑크박스. 나의 첫 아기 핑크박스. 까꿍 핑크박스. 요람에 넣고 흔들어보고픈 핑크박스. (참고로 말하지만 하나님은 네모난 것은 만들 줄 몰라.)...

Pinkbox that has just arrived. Pinkbox that waits to be opened. When I embrace the box, it smells of a faraway place. But no one who goes inside can escape. Ah adorable pinkbox. Pinkbox, my first baby. Hello, pinkbox. I want to rock pinkbox in a cradle. (For your information, God doesn't know how to make anything rectangular.)...

Fallen pinkbox. Torn pinkbox, pinkbox cast away, it might be better to grab onto the horizon. Can't embrace it since it has parted far. *Dirty pinkbox, smelly pinkbox, crumpled pinkbox, flowing pinkbox.* Pinkbox covered with faded writing, dirty pink, old pink, open hole pink, flapping, its hair down pink. Like a camera, pink captures you, but there is nothing after the film is taken out. Don't let the box return. It's just dirty paper. Burn this box.

—Kim Hyesoon, from "Pinkbox" in
All the Garbage of the World, Unite! (Action Books, 2011)

FREELY FRAYED

I'm not afraid, Free Trade! Kim Hyesoon dressed in pink, from top to bottom, and took part in the massive candlelight protests in Seoul, May and June of 2008. She sounded ecstatic in her emails, telling me about the spontaneous convergences of crowds, picnicking, playing music, dancing, singing against the lifting of the ban on U.S. beef as a pre-condition for the KORUS talks to begin again. This was not only about the safety of mighty U.S. beef, but also the dictatorial policies of the current government designed to appease its elites and the empire's demands. But it's all good, all good for the American shareholders. Even American shit is good, I hear. Tonight we'll line up to buy nutritious food scraps from the American bases. American lard melts then sizzles—we're making potato fritters for Papa's return from Vietnam. Tang Tang, we want Tang! Hey there, KORUS pokus, are you frayed? Pinkbox pinkbox, are you frayed? Hanky yankee, are you frayed?

• • •

See You Later Translator. No, I'm not an agitator. It turns out that I'm a mere imitator the lowly kind, which is none other than a translator, a mimicker of mimetic words in particular. Doubled consonants or certain parts of speech that are repeated on certain occasions, which can be said to be nobody's business, but they are since everything in English is everybody's business. *Farfar swiftswift zealzeal stuffstuff waddlewaddling stickysticky cacklecackled draindrained flowflow yellyell swishswish.* I've just been instructed to get rid of them by an evaluator, Why double up? No, I'm not a collaborator. I'm actually very frail, frailer than a Thumbelina in the world of everybody's business. In my world of nobody's business I twirl about frantically frequently farfar to the point of failure feigning englishenglish.

• • •

Pigspigs. Kim Hyesoon's animals are radical. They are given allegorical roles like the roles many animals have in Korean fables. According to many stories I heard as a child, a hundred-year-old fox can turn into a human or in some cases a fox that devours one hundred humans (some aim for human livers) can transform into a woman. These fox-women often trick children and seduce men in order to consume them. Men often encounter them at night during their travels away from the safety of their villages. The fox-women stand for evil women who are not fit to be dutiful wives, the fear of falling into danger, violence, and ingestion of bodily parts. In Kim Hyesoon's poem "Father is Heavy, What Do I Do?" a woman poet plays the role of a fox and *devour[s] one hundred fathers / and become[s] a father.* And *Father became a father because he'd killed father, his father's father.* The margin consumes the center and becomes the center. Kim's rats feast on human babies, adorable white rabbits, and also on one another and become rats again. In "Seoul's Dinner" Seoul is given the functions of ingestion and excretion: *Pigs enter. The pigs oink and suck on Seoul's lips…. Seoul, which is simultaneously a mouth and an anus.* Everything in its landscape enters and exits Seoul. Hence Seoul is always in the flux of becoming itself. In Shohei Imamura's film *Pigs and Battleship* (1961) local thugs, raising pigs for the GIs in Yokosuka where U.S. naval ships are stationed, are eating a cooked pig. The pig had previously consumed the body of a man the thugs had killed and disposed of at the pig farm. So when Imamura says he wanted to show the "power of pigs" by releasing hundreds of pigs into the GI streets of Yokosuka, the pigs become powerful pigs. They fill every alley, crushing everything in their way, and the thugs who have eaten the pigs are pigs, and the women in prostitution who prepare pigs for their Japanese male customers and GIs and eat pigs are also pigs. Yokosuka becomes a pig town. Kim's and Imamura's animals both instruct us how to subvert the order of power.

· · ·

Hailhail. I think of Kim Hyesoon's poems as being played out on a theatrical stage that has no regard for the conventions of linear narrative time. Her time is radical. There is no before or after hell. Every minute is hell. Every minute piles up like *teeth with teeth, fingernails with fingernails*. Kim's hell is rooted in the Korean shaman narrative, *The Abandoned*, in which a daughter is abandoned for being a daughter—the seventh daughter to be born in a row to a king. Princess Abandoned goes on a journey to the realm of death and returns to her place of origin to save her dying parents, becoming a spirit who guides the dead to another realm. Kim's feminist reading of this narrative is that Princess Abandoned's realm of death is not an oppressed space but a counter-patriarchal one where a woman can redefine herself. In this place, *a woman, the empty darkness, does not follow the logic of ownership*. Princess Abandoned's hell is a *black mirror*. Kim's hell extends from this black mirror, remaining counter-patriarchal, possessing nothing, reflecting and resisting *Mr. Military Officers with black ink*. Hence, *the darkness inside Seoul's intestines is dense*. Forever empty, Kim's miniature stages stack up and shatter with their weight of emptiness the militarized borders. It is August 6, 1945. The time is 8:14 AM. Hair hails down. Hairy hell. In Shohei Imamura's *Black Rain* (1989) time never really moves beyond the time of the Hiroshima atomic bomb explosion because the image of the clock persists throughout the film. This is how we know the black rain is still falling inside the survivors, and this is why translation must also persist like Imamura's clock to remind us of the hell within and outside of the U.S. empire. Oh, wait, let's hail, *teeth with teeth, fingernails with fingernails*.

· · ·

Failfail. One August, I interpret for a woman at a shelter, downstairs from where I teach. She'd come from South Korea four months ago. She stayed in Los Angeles for two months and when she could no longer pay her $350-a-month rent, she took a bus up to Seattle and began living on the street. She is not certain if she has ever been arrested. She remembers that she shouted something loud on the street in Los Angeles and was approached by a police officer. She is not certain if that means she was arrested. She is surrounded by people who are given orders to stalk her by someone hiding in the darkness. Whenever she decides to do something, the people who follow orders prevent her from doing what she wants to do. She says they have no basic knowledge of being human. She feels they are capable of doing something harmful. Her parents are deceased and her siblings have their own lives and families. She used to work in factories. She is divorced. She would like to enroll in a school to study ESL. She would like to know if she can really start studying English soon. As a translator I am preoccupied with home—my first home, South Korea—and things that are dislocated from home. For me, translation is a process of perpetual displacement, one set of linguistic signs displaced by another. And this displacement takes place under specific historical conditions, sometimes acting out the orders from the darkness. My translation takes orders from Kim Hyesoon's hell that defies neocolonial orders. The displaced poetic identity persists in its dislocation, translating itself out of the orders of darkness through the translator, another displaced identity. We have no choice but to *failfail. Failingfailing*, it's painful becoming a translation, becoming an immigrant. One August, I find the woman in the lunchroom of the shelter. She is very troubled by the people who follow her. She has told them they are worthless beings, yet they don't react at all. She doesn't understand how they could be so indifferent to such a remark. She repeats, "Worthless beings? Worthless beings?" When translation fails, displaced identities easily become worthless beings.

• • •

So what makes Kim Hyesoon a radical poet? Prior to the early twentieth century, Korean women's poetry existed primarily within the oral tradition. Women were restricted from learning the written language, which was then classical Chinese, except for Korean script, *hangŭl*, a writing system promulgated in 1446 for women and commoners. The written literary realm was dominated by men and still is. Women poets of the 1920s were able to publish their poetry for the first time, but for many decades—five decades to be exact—Korean women's poetry was characterized by a language of passivity and contemplation that was predefined by men. It wasn't till the late 1970s that a women's poetry energized by feminist consciousness and innovation began to challenge the status quo. Kim Hyesoon first published in 1979 in a prominent journal called *Literature and Intellect*. And her first book of poems, *From Another Star*, was published in 1981. So this is why she is often referred to as a poet of the 80s. She also belongs to the *hangŭl* generation, a generation that was educated in the Korean script. An older generation like my father's was educated in Japanese and his father's generation in classical Chinese. Kim along with poets such as Ch'oe Sŭng-ja and Yi Yŏn-ju (the two other poets I translated in my anthology, *Anxiety of Words*) challenged and resisted the prescribed literary conventions for women.

Sunsusi (pure poetry) and *ch'amyŏsi* (engaged poetry) are the two trends that have dominated modern Korean poetry, and Kim Hyesoon was the first woman poet to receive the *Kim Su-yông* and *Midang* poetry awards named after poets who represent the two dominant trends. Radical is not the word Koreans use for Kim Hyesoon. Korean critics (but not all—many still dismiss her poetry) are very well aware that she is radical in her poetic, linguistic innovations, but she is simply referred to as a "modern" poet. And her poetry is not often perceived as political. To be perceived as a political poet you must have been associated with *minjok* or *minjung munhak* (national/people's literature), which dominated the literary scene during the dictatorship of the 70s and 80s. The only organization Kim has belonged to is Another Culture, a feminist organization that was primarily responsible for establishing women's studies in South Korea and for the publication of feminist criticism. So Kim Hyesoon finds it very amusing, when she reads certain reviews written by U.S. critics, that her poetry is perceived as being political. This is partly due to the way I have framed her poetry. And I will continue to do so because her poetry and translation of her poetry take place within the neocolonial context of South Korea and the U.S. We are always at the risk of becoming worthless beings or radical *failfail*.

FROM *SOUTH OF THE LINE ("ALOHA ACTIVITIES")*

MELANIE RANDS

Honolulu Star Advertiser Monday 5/2/11
The text of President Obama's speech to the nation.

OF INNOCENCE AND NEARLY

tonight we give thanks by firefight and slaughter to the worst images against our country and so shortly after taking justice through a cloud-less sky I met repeatedly with professionals and destruction. on a good and historic day we tolerate the cause of our frayed national memory yet we will be true just as the pursuit of justice develops more innocent men and women to make the killing or shortly after. we will be true even as we develop more national memory the story of our history is testament to the greatness of an operation that our citizens and friends and those that were darkened against us to make the world a safer place. we are once again reminded of the priority of our efforts along that border, the heroic work of our team on that bright september day collapsing to the ground as we do whatever it takes to make the killing. then after painstaking unity and the blood of innocent neighbors, we must and we will feel the satisfaction that has borne part of a generation to make the world a place of prosperity, of war, nor stand idle. I directed our citizens to stand up. to stand up after a certain time and do whatever it takes. we will never tolerate sacrifices to mark the end of securing our country not just because of wealth or power. and so shortly after they took care to avoid casualties it took many months to run this thread to capture or kill the cost of sacrifice I've made clear he was a mass murderer. we quickly learn the story of our history on nights like this was far from the murder of thousands. we offered the wounded our blood and going forward the death does not mark the end of our effort. meanwhile the greatness of our country unseen along that border is a testament those that were children will remain vigilant of his body. with my team, with my demise by all who look into the eyes of justice we give thanks because of who we are. we are once again the story of our values abroad. let me say to the families this is a good and historic day that has borne a message to prevent another attack to protect our empty table.

Ravishing hyperrealism
Ecstatic ascetiscism
Multi process tracking shot
Interactive multi dimensionality
Mind blowing
Baudrillard, *America* p31

UP THE GULLY

[voice 1]

a blue plastic tarp
keeps the wood dry
it's been raining
& the sky's grey
as far as you can see

The kikuyu's growing .

& ever since the warranty ran out
the fridge makes a knocking sound

if you squint
it could be a tug boat engine
a long way off

but most of the time
we don't squint

we finish unpacking the car
and I squat down
& mark my territory
like a dog

cabbage tree leaves
& big wet puka leaves
cover the grass

we'll have to rake those
before we mow

there on the wall is the clock
we brought back
from your mums

| after |

she looks so young
in her nurse's uniform
in that photo on the shelf

| before |

her head tilts
& she turns to stone

& the lichen ticks
& the puriri makes a hollow knocking sound
& the spiders purr

The kikuyu's growing .

someone's been using our
torches and gumboots

they're not by the door
where we left them

UP THE GULLY

[voice 2]

we got this place
with a mortgage
& a swanndri handshake

he said tell your fulla's fulla
to talk to my fulla

most of the bush was cleared way back
to make way for pasture
& kikuyu invaded every dry crack
of the bare hills & river flats

there were no roads
just a farm track
cutting across
the paddocks

the manuka came back first
then pittosporums, coprosmas
cabbage trees & nikau
kauri, rimu, totara & kahikatea

The kikuyu's growing .

& we just got here
& it's time to go

GOING NOISES

down on your marks to keep
going but for a long time
the sun beats the top off nowhere
like Neil Armstrong reaching for a coke

my hat for the stars
but all over this park
the grass stains on my knees
are howling **Too many!**

30 silver feet on the ground
on your hush hush high and
the trickle of **go go go!**
as barefoot athletics and t.v.

the onehunga weed prickles
we're down on 30 elbows
and getting hotter for gold
but forever doesn't

I shouldn't kill for the weight of guns
like god going off at capable clipboards
in prideaux park
                            until next time

SQUEEZE!

the feijoas shuffle
in the april shake down

dropping long before they're ready
to the

                                     ground

found by knives and fingers and lips and tongues

      squeeze !
      s-q-u-e-e-z-e !
      my hoo-ha-esss !

the feijoas kerfuffle
their sucked out skins

and tingling tart-ness
left undone

in backyard s
of
idyl tenderness

for
        mice and birds and ants and other   insects

ace lina lina rice
call a cry
cry in lieu
run a yell
yell a clue
race a year
a lunar yen
acul in ary alien

SHIPS LOG:

6pm is a highlighter bumper sticker on an
SUV at the lights telling you

not all those who wander are

lost

so we keep turning left
until we find a place to park the car
and eat our fish and chips
with the windows
rolled down

lying on the jetty at your uncles
bach on Rangitoto
your hands floating on the water
waiting for the crawlies to
come and nibble your fingers

SHIPS LOG: 6pm at the celestial lights
we were looking for polaris
we were following the signs
we were wishing for a monkeys fist
on a heaving line
so we kept turning right until

we found ourselves lost
and

pushingoutthroughthecrowd

SHIPS LOG:

In the Mid Pacific area north west from the Marquesas I came to an island.

NURABAR
ROTUMA H.
ALICE

(Lady)

American

× Ratu Rabici (Kambermi).   Ratu Pope
                             Hitcheson
Rarawai
Marama.
Rani   (Sugar co.)
Confiánsa
Addy Keva I
Andy Keva II   ~~Ratal~~ Malaqa.
Andy Rewa
~~I~~

Sir John Forrest
Tui Kauvaro
Tui Cakau.   (Retired). Uncle Dutch.
S.T. 44.   Uncle Dutch
KIA KIA   ×   P. 391.
ADi MERE
PURPLE SEA.

TONAIA.

FIJIAN PRINCESS

TUI VALAIALA.

DEGEI.

when the boat comes down
a dadakulaci lies unconscious on the ground
4 nights of singing the horizon away

the banana boat swinging
16 knots into diesel sunsets

on twin Armstrong-Sulzer 6 cylinder engines
Bob 'Gin' rocking her golden whiskey cabin for
3 days straight

the night my father came

with 2000 tonnes of ripening cargo
her quota of islanders bursting
to
over

f
l
o
w

kai vulagi on the bunks & everyone else down below
all their spirits rolled into one

the night my father came
with whales teeth and a turtle shell
on the Matua

all 355.2 feet of her round
cape brett and up the
Rangitoto channel

when the boat comes down

to Mrs Harveys boarding house on
Hepburn Street in Free man's Bay

a gas stove and a double bed
in her refrigerated hold

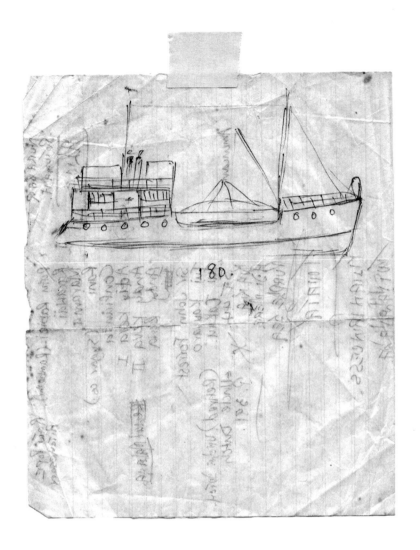

tides

         red   feather

            native

daughter

                   shoe

Pearls
During half an hours fishing a
native diver brought up for me eight oysters
averaging nine inches in breadth
and from these four small pearls
were secured

Fanning Island lying in the pacific ocean latitude 3°
and 4° North, longitude159° and 160° West

SHIPS LOG:

We finished taking in cargo, silver sand and boxes of earth.
At noon set sail. East wind, fresh. Crew, five hands ... two mates, cook, and myself
(captain).
(Captains Log. Bram Stoker's Dracula)

San Francisco to Fanning Island
Greig resided in San Francisco for some years. When he died, in compliance with his expressed wish he was buried on Fanning Island. Greig was an ardent Freemason, and the brethren in San Francisco were determined that although his wish should be respected as to his interment on Fanning Island his remains should be interred in consecrated ground.

Greig's Brig, the Douglas, which had remained in San Francisco for many months, was fitted up for the purpose and some hundred tons of soil taken from a consecrated graveyard was placed in her hold. In this the grave was dug and the last rites were carried out with full masonic honours. The Douglas sailed for F. Island and the reinterment was carried out with equal solemnity.

Evening Post, Volume LXXI, Issue 76, 30 March 1906 page 5

SHIPS LOG:

On 16 July mate reported in the morning that one of the crew was missing. Could not account for it. Took larboard watch eight bells last night, was relieved by 'A', but did not go to bunk. Men more downcast than ever. All said they expected something of the kind, but would not say more than there was SOMETHING aboard. Mate getting very impatient with them. Feared some trouble ahead.

Do you ne'er forget the glory
Of the gorgeous tropic blooms
Do you never long again to see
The golden blossomed broom
Or the beech, the birch, and hazel
And the graceful rowan tree
Or the gowan and the daisy
Or the star-bespangled lea.

Had the boat been upset the
sharks, with which these waters
abound, would have made short
work of the daring sailor.

the voice of the percer tells me there's a reading light
located on the panel above my head

above my head the keep-seatbelts-fastened-at-all-times light
comes on as we are encountering some turbulence

there is turbulence back home when a tornado
lifts the roof off a shopping mall in Albany

flight NZ9 lifts off the runway in Honolulu
as I reach up to switch on my overhead light

           atoll

                                    lagoon
                 date line

                 musician

The word "Matua" is common to most Polynesian languages and usually means "kinship." In New Zealand and around the Islands she was popularly referred to as "the banana boat."

I came to New Zealand in May 1945, I remember the Niagra had struck a mine and sunk. Another steamer going around the Pacific at that time was the Matua. Overcrowding wasn't uncommon in wartime and the Matua usually had too many passengers.

The gymnasium on board was full of women and girls. I slept on the floor in a cabin with 2 bunks; there were 2 pakeha's on the bunks. One of them was a guy nicknamed Bob 'Gin'. His wife had left him because he drank too much and he was coming out to New Zealand to see her after promising he'd given it up. He had a case of whiskey under his bunk and was drunk most of the time. He spent one night unconscious on the toilet floor.

The map is not the territory

FROM *THE ROMANCE OF SIAM*

JAI ARUN RAVINE

WHITE LOVE[1]

Why Thailand? I literally looked through the, the catalog once
and, um, as soon as I, I saw the, the word Thailand
I, I knew. It's sort of a, strange
feeling, um, to explain. But I, I went out that night and bought a,
uh, culture shock book, um, on Thailand, read it in about
three hours and decided that, you know, everything
about the culture of the people, the history of the place
is something that I, I needed to explore on my own.

I, I have never owned the place of my, um, mother's birth. I, I visited there once, twice and I, I want to apply for the, uh, Fulbright, too. I, I've read literally everything White people have written about, um, Thailand but I, I wasn't prepared for the, uh, shock of being too, um, White, too American, too, you know, strange

for Thai people. It's sort of a, um, strange feeling for me too, Paige, that you can own the experience of, uh, being there and no one's, you know, shocked about it. Everyone else has been to Thailand at least once: The People Are So Nice. And The Food!!! I, I see the word Thailand written on overpriced imported coconut milk cans, uh,

everything except my body has the mark. Your life, and everything in it changed for you and, um, nothing changed for me. I, I'm a stranger in a place I, I thought was mine. *Lonely Planet Thailand* says the Kingdom of, um, Thailand draws more visitors than any other country in Southeast Asia, while its, you know, own people are drawn to Europe, to study French, and not once do they miss the, uh, virtually irresistible combination of shocking

---

1 DID YOU KNOW? This destination features lines from Paige Battcher's interview on the "My Fulbright Life" podcast, September 9, 2010.
INFORMATION: The Thai title of Apichatpong Weerasethakul's film *Tropical Malady* (2004) is สัตว์ประหลาด ("strange creature").

grandeur and ruin. Culture, um, shock works in many different ways, Paige. I, I pretended I, I couldn't speak English, suppressed everything non-Thai so I, I could, you know, belong? Once my, um, mother said, I, I've lived with strangers all my life, one more won't make a difference. I, I was on my own reading the word, um,

Thailand in books in order to learn about myself, but Thailand *loves* and, uh, *accepts* you without *question* and I, I'm in shock and I, I don't think I, I will, you know, recover, ever. I, I want my own Fulbright Life. I, I want to steal everything you took. *Tropical Malady* or "Strange Creature," um, that's what I, I am. Once

and forever, not just Once In A Lifetime, I,
I want to experience, um, Thailand—
the strange feeling of, uh, amazing shock
to discover that, you know, everything I am
a White person owns.

THE ROMANCE OF THE SIAMESE DREAM[2]

OVERTURE

In a world between reality and imagination,
a woman creates a fiction to cover up her past
and a man creates a character that will forever change his future.

Will they become who they are meant to be?
Only the romance of the dream will tell.

ACT ONE

YUL BRYNNER is having one of his recurring dreams.

He's on stage for the 4,634th performance of THE KING AND I.

The theatre is deserted. All the work lights and house lights are on.

It's hot.

A traveling spotlight is trained on him.

YUL paces, barefoot, to the proscenium. The spotlight follows.

YUL paces, barefoot, to the scrim. The spotlight follows.

---

2 HIGHLIGHTS: Yul Brynner performed the role of the King in *The King and I* approximately 4,633 times during the course of his lifetime. He was known to make up stuff about his life in interviews, like saying he was descended from Genghis Khan. The real Anna Leonowens was born in Bombay in working class military camps; her mother was most likely mixed race (half South Asian, half White). At some point in her life Anna decided to rewrite her past and told people she was born in England and was an upper class Englishwoman. Everyone believed her—even her grandchildren. The author is intrigued by the way these two people reinvented their lives, and how the characters they brought to life are wrapped up in *The King and I* saga.
DID YOU KNOW? This piece was written while listening to the Smashing Pumpkins *Siamese Dream* (1993) album.

YUL paces, barefoot, to the wing stage right. The spotlight doesn't follow.

Thinking he's free of it, YUL turns his back on the spot, which immediately makes a beeline for him.

YUL swears he can hear the light chuckle.

A large rice cooker appears stage center. Its top is open. It is clean and empty. The electric cord spills out of its side. The metal is buzzing.

In the dream the rice cooker tells YUL its name is TIGER.

YUL paces up to TIGER, barefoot, exposes his chest, raises his brow, points his finger.

TIGER (telepathically): Wow, I'm so not impressed.

YUL (emphatically): Go on go on go on!

TIGER (telepathically): OK, so ... I'm a wormhole. I didn't show up last time you had this dream, so if I were you, I'd take a ride.

YUL can feel TIGER's hot breath.

TIGER wants YUL to come inside.

YUL gingerly inserts his bald head into the cooker. He sheds his silk jacket, his silk fisherman pants, and his two gold anklets.

ACT TWO

YUL emerges out on the other side. He's on stage again. The house lights and work lights are out. All the spots are focused on him, blinding white. He's sitting on the floor, knees drawn up to his chin, naked and hairless.

TIGER is gone. In TIGER's place is ANNA. The REAL ANNA Leonowens from THE KING AND I. ANNA is wearing a giant hoop skirt that fills two-thirds of the stage. She's wearing a strange brooch set with two tiger claws. She's here to teach YUL the art of acting.

ANNA (dismissively): What a child you are.

YUL (defensively): I used to be a boy. What I choose is my choice.

ANNA (excitedly): Do you want to pretend? Do you want to play a game of make-believe?

Backstage the dressing rooms are filled with white underwear and metal forks, all in disarray. ANNA directs YUL to go clean it up.

YUL is sweating. He can't stack up all the forks perfectly, they keep slipping and falling. When YUL folds one pair of underwear, three more appear.

ANNA (inquisitively): Do you want to change your name?

YUL (decisively): People don't know my real self, and they're not about to find out!

At the proscenium appears a railing. ANNA and YUL lean on it and look out into the audience.

ANNA (reminiscing): I came to America from the same port as the Titanic. And I ...

YUL (with gusto, completing ANNA's sentence): ... and I am the King of Siam!

YUL feels slightly ridiculous, like he's in a blockbuster movie.

ANNA (in the manner of good advice): Reinvent yourself the moment you disembark.

ACT THREE

ANNA directs YUL to stop organizing the underwear and forks backstage and make a living poem out of it.

Instead, YUL writes a dead letter to ANNA's grandmother.

YUL (poetically):

> Dear Sleeping Dictionary,
> Won't you wake?
> I need to look up the word, "Character."

Army, British Bombay. Where is
The Company?
Uncle Tom,
Cousin Tom,
Husband Tom,
Sleeping Tom.
Penang, Prince of Wales.

The stage turns into a raft on the river, secured to the shore by ropes and chains.

ANNA (nostalgically): I wrote my biography in eight pages. My grandchildren believed every word of it. All it requires is that you act the part.

YUL (apprehensively): So, I pretend to be someone I want to be...

ANNA (definitively): ...and I finally become that person, or she becomes me.

FINALE (ULTIMO)

ANNA stares at YUL with entire singleness of eye. In thirty seconds YUL grows a full head of hair that keeps growing down to the floor, across the stage, into the aisles. In thirty seconds ANNA has progressed to old age and is going blind. Her dark, deep-set eyes turn into balls of hard white wax.

UNDER ERASURE

Note: This essay has been reconstituted from blog entries originally written during March and April 2011. I was invited to do a residency at ComPeung Village of Creativity in Doi Saket, Thailand, and the short film I created there, TOM / TRANS / THAI, *was exhibited as part of "Chiang Mai Now!" at the Bangkok Art and Culture Centre. Since then, the short film has screened at Anarchopride 2014 (Stockholm), Entzaubert 2014 (Berlin), Sabina Lee Gallery (Los Angeles), and CAAMFest 2013 (San Francisco), among others. This essay is a more informal window into my daily experiences making the film, as I grapple with issues of gender, race and language. For a fuller and more formal view on this subject, please see my critical article that accompanies the film, "Toms and Zees: Locating FTM Identity in Thailand," published in* Transgender Studies Quarterly *Issue 1.3 (Duke University Press, 2014).*

WEEK 1 [DOI SAKET] (MARCH 16, 2011)

It's already the end of my first week at ComPeung, an artist-in-residence program in Doi Saket outside Chiang Mai, Thailand. It's a short bicycle ride around the lake into Doi Saket market, the cafe with Wi-Fi and 7-Eleven. On my first day I flew kites and fell full-on into the rice paddy ditch—my muddy "welcome back" Thai baptism. It's been seven years since my first visit to Thailand and this time I'm prepared—prepared for being read as *farang*, prepared to say *khrap*—ready to work.

ComPeung invited me to create my short experimental film *TOM / TRANS / THAI* for the "Chiang Mai Now!" art exhibition, which opens April 7, 2011 at the Bangkok Art and Culture Centre and runs through June. My goal is to bring the cultural categories of *tom* and FTM transgender into conversation among Thai nationals and Thai Americans through interviews with Thai *toms* and Thai transmasculine folk and my response to those interviews.

So far I have been interviewed by *Gavroche*, a French magazine in Bangkok, by folks making a documentary on the art exhibition, and by *Citylife Chiang Mai* magazine for their upcoming May issue on "the body." I will be presenting the film and my related research at the April 19 Informal Northern Thai Group meeting in Chiang Mai, and perhaps a couple other places. Additionally, I recently had a paper related to the project accepted for presentation at the Thai Studies Conference in Bangkok at the end of July.

It seems that many folks are interested in the work I am trying to do, in the sense that a discourse around Thai *tom* and transmasculine identity (relative to *sao praphet song* and transfeminine identity) is in the early stages of being built. Returning to Thailand as a transmasculine person is the ultimate in "self-building," as Bo Luengsuraswat writes. In this project I am reaching through our isolation and alienation as Thai American transmasculine people and Thai American queers and building a community for each other.

For the past few days it's been very rainy, highly unusual for this time of year, which has been putting me in a miserable mood. Fortunately I was finally able to interview one of my participants this morning on Skype and now I'm feeling up. With a good dose of *@tom act* (Bangkok's tomboy lifestyle magazine) and pop star Zee Matanawee Keenan's music videos, I'm already forgetting about the bike ride home in the rain.

WEEK 2 [DOI SAKET] (MARCH 19, 2011)

I went to pay respects to the Buddha at a meditation center, which obviously didn't work out. I dropped my flipcam there and now it won't turn on. Extremely annoyed at having paid USD $200 for such a piece of shit, the only things curing my mood are the clear skies and Skyping with genderqueer Thais on the other side of the world. Friends, I wish I could bring you here.

It's Ostara, and the weekend-long temple fair, and the time when the Moon is full and as close as it will get to Earth. Amidst booming night music and flying termites I feel a bit frantic, overwhelmed and in need of solitary work space in which to process the conversations I've had with participants so far.

The windy country road out to Doi Saket hot spring reminds me of West Virginia again. I often feel nagging periods of *déjà vu* and the quickly arising normality of my day to day, with insect-bite-swollen feet to prove it. Yesterday I ate ant eggs (*kai mot*) and am enjoying *sit ua* and *ahan nuea*—the food of the north.

At Chiang Mai Airport Plaza, I passed the TOM professional laycut barbershop. In the B2S (Books, Music, Stationery), the first song that came on was by Calories Blah Blah from the soundtrack to *Bangkok Love Story* (a gay Thai film)—"I want to know, but I don't want to ask." I found issue 24 of *@tom act*, for which I eagerly paid 125 baht. I looked for Zee's VCDs and a copy of the Thai *tom/dee* film *Yes or No*, but couldn't find them.

As Thai American transmasculine folk, we live with separation, dissonance, ambivalence and constant negotiation. I read *tom* identity as transmasculine, but translating transmasculinity as a concept or an experience to other *tom*-identified folk is maybe impossible. However, the discovery of the existence of *@tom act* and Zee have helped me uncover a space for my own embodiment of genderqueer-ness and Thai-ness—they opened the gate.

Inside is a restaurant where we can all meet together to eat. Here our Thai-ness and genderqueer-ness are not exoticized. Here we are free to have our own "tastes," whether rice, sticky rice or bread. Here we are neither gendered nor pressured to gender ourselves. Here language does not demand we make ourselves visible, unless we choose to do so.

Here, you know the food will be really good.

WEEK 3 [DOI SAKET] (MARCH 28, 2011)

Aftershocks from the earthquake in Burma, rain forebodes yet again, but my camera is actually working. Anyways...

This Friday a draft of my short film is due for review by the exhibition folks. Even with nearly 20 minutes of footage gathered in a rough edit, part of me feels like I barely started. I'm overwhelmed by the task of synthesizing the material I've gathered so far and teasing out the text I want to highlight in the film from the larger paper I'm writing. I want to visually represent the complexity of our experiences in the film, despite the fact that sometimes it feels like there really are only two ways to turn when you reach the road.

I met some folks in the administration at Payap University, where I studied abroad in 2004, and saw how much the campus has changed and grown. I will hopefully be presenting the film and project to some students there near the end of April. Additionally, the Library of Congress Bangkok office emailed me wanting to acquire a copy of the film. I said, "Well, it isn't finished yet..."

We went to a restaurant in town to meet a worker there who might be interested in being interviewed for the project. A person who I think was their partner walked me around the corner to a *tom* working on a computer. She asked them if they wanted to be interviewed and they basically said, "No! I'm not interested," and kept working. Too bad though—they were super hot.

FYI: There are too many white people in Chiang Mai. I am incredibly glad to be avoiding the 24/7/365 tourist vay-cay party zone for now, and am feeling quite at home in Doi Saket, the gay country boi that I am. I don't know that there are really people here who I can befriend outside the restrictions of language and gender, who can really understand my kind of queerness. But downloading the rest of Zee's songs and watching the new video on repeat make me feel like this virtual desire could be a start.

WEEK 4 [BANGKOK] (APRIL 9, 2011)

Taking the night train down to Bangkok, I have a heaviness in my heart. At 6:00AM the outskirts of the metropolis slide by—shacks, station platforms—and I think: Who am I, to be "representing" Thai-ness? To be "representing" tom-ness? When the faces of Thais on the BTS—bored, vacant, watching commercials on flat screen TVs, many of whom I read as *tom*—come into proximity without any recognition. I am "from" this. That morning I didn't want it.

My film *TOM / TRANS / THAI* is installed now as part of the "Chiang Mai Now!" exhibition at the Bangkok Art and Culture Centre (BACC) in one corner of the 9th floor. I feel insecure about the ways my difference is marked in the show—as American, as genderqueer, as half Thai. My body inhabits the screen, carrying the vulnerability of my experience and the experiences of each person I interviewed.

I don't think that a dialogue between *tom* and transgender men in Thailand has yet to reach popular discourse. Every Thai transmasculine person I talked to said they didn't know any other Thai trans guys—and every *tom* I talked to didn't know any transgender men, besides the odd newspaper or TV story. What I begin to do here, with this film, is open that door, to connect us. To remove the hinge. I don't attempt to define "art."

Out of place, perhaps. But yesterday I went back to the BACC to meet one of the project participants. We sat on the bean bag chairs and, without speaking, my experience of watching myself, this time, was filled with so much warmth, knowing I was sitting next to someone who understood, who cared, who shared in the complexity and pain and unspokenness of what I chose to visually represent.

My new friend (new brother) and I walked and talked, around the 9th floor, down and outside, across the BTS bridge and over into Siam Square, through sidewalks packed with planters meant to deter the vendors who packed around the planters anyway, discovering we like to walk and like parks and carry water bottles, and that

Thai people don't like walking and don't like parks and don't carry water bottles. Are we still Thai, or what? We got a Singha at the 7-Eleven and sat on the posts outside talking even more. I was filled with so much joy—so much joy. To know myself, here.

After my friend and I departed I wandered back, stumbling upon a "Hello! Korea" audition in front of the MBK mall. From the BTS bridge I watched boys in tight jeans and high tops rehearse their dance routines, and I thought—Bangkok, Krungtep, *this*—this part I take as mine.

WEEK 5 [CHIANG MAI] (APRIL 14, 2011)

When I asked for internet, I didn't ask for internet + mosquitoes. Although internet + steak, internet + massage and internet + coffee are all readily available. I can't get a date with a human, but bugs are into me. Mosquitoes, beetles, flying termites—all up in my grill.

Renting a room in Chiang Mai during Songkran, Thai New Year, is maybe one of the most difficult things to do. The only tasks more difficult? Staying dry, and avoiding wet hippies. I walk out of G.G. Somphet guest house in my fluorescent orange poncho with only one agenda: Banana smoothie.

It's true. *Farang* LOVE smoothies. They also love chalkboards with color-coded listings of Fresh Dragonfruit, Kiwi and Pineapple. But I like smoothies too. And the woman in the market sells Banana smoothies for only 15 baht. So as I approach in my orange poncho the *farang* convention in front of her stall, waiting for their yogurt and muesli, I feel embarrassed. 15 baht, I tell myself. 15 baht.

This week I've been hiding out. Recovering from the midnight bus ride from Bangkok to Chiang Mai, which sped through a massive lightning and thunderstorm with some small-scale flooding, and avoiding water fights. I'm also working on my presentation for next Tuesday's Informal Northern Thai Group meeting.

It's not that I haven't felt like celebrating. Since the earthquake and tsunami in Japan, weather in Thailand just hasn't been the same. It's cold, rainy and cloudy, and I didn't come to Thailand to wear my requisite Bay Area black hoodie. It's supposed to be the hot season, people. Drinking beer and slinging buckets of canal water in the street (while it's raining) is not my idea of a great time.

This Sunday is my 28th birthday, and I remember, vaguely, the kind of person I was seven years ago, when I turned 21 in Chiang Mai and had a tequila sunrise in a gay bar, none of which was particularly special. It's called grenadine, my friend said. I accidentally walked away with a purple napkin from that restaurant, now stained with seven years of snot.

As I walk back to my room with 10 baht bags of watermelon and papaya, my orange poncho one giant force-field against nonconsensual water-throwing, I think, I really do want to love Thailand like all the white people do. I really wish I could. But as they fade in and out of view in heterosexual groupings and hefty super soakers, their wet flip-flops squishing on tile, I kind of feel like this city, this whole country, should just be theirs. Go ahead. Enjoy yourself.

WEEK 6 [CHIANG MAI] (APRIL 25, 2011)

"Under erasure." I was reading Aren Z. Aizura's essay "Where Health and Beauty Meet: Femininity and Racialisation in Thai Cosmetic Surgery Clinics" in *Asian Studies Review* 33.3, when I stumbled upon this "Derridean term to denote using a word when it does not quite fit, but acknowledging the impossibility of finding the 'correct' word or pinning down meaning absolutely" (Aizura, Notes).

I first encountered Derrida in Akilah Oliver's "Eros and Loss in Poetic Construction" seminar during my graduate studies at Naropa University's Jack Kerouac School. We were reading *Aporias*. Recently Akilah was in my dream, and it was as if she actually hadn't died. We were opening the lock on a door to a secret part of her apartment, the place where she had stayed.

Before traveling to Thailand, I drew the Goddess cards Ianna, Venus and Hel. These last few weeks I've realized the great effort needed just to break the surface. Each day spirits lead me through the underworld, up through the politics of representation and vulnerability, across constant investigation and negotiation, opening up some secret way.

Last Tuesday I showed the film and gave a talk at an Informal Northern Thai Group meeting at the Alliance Française. In order for people to understand what I was talking about, I spent a lot of time defining terminology. FTM, MTF, transmasculine, transfeminine, transgender, cisgender, se/hir. Most people in Thailand ask, "Why are you categorizing people? Why are you putting them into boxes? Are you seeking definition for yourself? Here, people go with the flow."

I say: I'm seeking a space outside binary thinking. I want to question the silence, invisibility and isolation of Thai transgender men and transmasculine folks. I want to look at the failure of language in conceptualizing and communicating who we are in the Thai cultural context.

Aizura writes, "...as a standard-bearer for Thai nationalism....The feminine body is often the site at which the conflicts arising from this straddling of tradition and modernity play out. From the perspective of the non-Thai tourist, these same images of 'Thai beauty' represent a form of idealised femininity that is both desired as exotic and cultural appropriated or 'eaten.'"

Is the silence around the existence of Thai transgender men due to the ways we reject and/or refigure this Thai nationalist feminine ideal? Is it because we cannot be commodified?

I want to know about Akilah's question, "What is the primary duty of repair?"

The poverty of language, but I'm still speaking. Still seeking to articulate a vocabulary.

Under erasure, but I'm still standing. Still making meaning.

WEEK 7 [CHIANG MAI] (MAY 2, 2011)

When I tried to register for the Thai Studies Conference, I got an "Error Gid." This is what happens when you are required to select either "Professor," "Associate Professor," "Assistant Professor," "Dr.," "Mr.," "Mrs." or "Ms." and all you have is an MFA.

Last week I bought my train ticket down to Bangkok, and the person behind the counter selected "MAN" without asking. I say *khrap*, usually quietly, not really expecting people to take me seriously. Even though they didn't check IDs last time, I'm still anxious about whether I should be passing as male today, and triply anxious about whether I'll pass as female for tomorrow night's journey through airport security. Last time, I was asked "Is this you?" of my passport photo. *Twice.* It's from 2003. I had really long hair.

From SFO to BKK I was "Ms." at the check-in counter, "Ma'am" in the security body scan chamber, "Sir" when I was waved through for boarding and "Sir" when I wanted some orange juice. In Suvarnabhumi I used the women's toilet, trying to not make eye contact with anyone, a white kid staring at me the whole time.

I don't like passing as male, and it's been hard these past two months accepting the reality that, when people aren't looking at my ID, I do. I don't feel male, I don't feel like anything. Meaning, I don't feel like either. I feel like a man joiner.

Thailand is made out of plastic bags and 7-Eleven. White people love it here. White people never want to leave. I'll miss the soya bean milk/fruit shake stall boy and the *kao mun gai* stall and the *kanom si grok* from Warorot Market. But I'm Thai and I'm White and I'm ready to go.

FROM *ALL THE IDENTITY ANSWERS*

YA-WEN HO

This list is written by a list-maker.

This list is written by a list-maker; a zinester; a fosterer of cats; a lover of sunny days; a left-hander; a ticklish person; a drinker of tea; a wearer of patterned tights.

This list is written by a list-maker; a zinester; a fosterer of cats; a lover of sunny days; a left-hander; a ticklish person; a drinker of tea; a wearer of patterned tights; a frequenter of second-hand shops; a dedicated recycler; a frugal person; a grower of vegetables; a lazy cook; a feeder of chickens.

This list is written by a list-maker; a zinester; a fosterer of cats; a lover of sunny days; a left-hander; a ticklish person; a drinker of tea; a wearer of patterned tights; a frequenter of second-hand shops; a dedicated recycler; a frugal person; a grower of vegetables; a lazy cook; a feeder of chickens; a polydactyl cat's human; an omnivore; a person with size 5 feet; a person who always has to hem their pants; a six-toe-nailed person; a person with no piercings; a person with an accidental tattoo.

This list is written by a list-maker; a zinester; a fosterer of cats; a lover of sunny days; a left-hander; a ticklish person; a drinker of tea; a wearer of patterned tights; a frequenter of second-hand shops; a dedicated recycler; a frugal person; a grower of vegetables; a lazy cook; a feeder of chickens; a polydactyl cat's human; an omnivore; a person with size 5 feet; a person who always has to hem their pants; a six-toe-nailed person; a person with no piercings; a person with an accidental tattoo; a doodler; a feather-weight drunk; a queen of vehicular slumber; a flirt; a dark-haired person; a dark-eyed person; a Sagittarian.

This list is written by a list-maker; a zinester; a fosterer of cats; a lover of sunny days; a left-hander; a ticklish person; a drinker of tea; a wearer of patterned tights; a frequenter of second-hand shops; a dedicated recycler; a frugal person; a grower of vegetables; a lazy cook; a feeder of chickens; a polydactyl cat's human; an omnivore; a person with size 5 feet; a person who always has to hem their pants; a six-toe-nailed person; a person with no piercings; a person with an accidental tattoo; a doodler; a feather-weight drunk; a queen of vehicular slumber; a flirt; a dark-haired person; a dark-eyed person; a Sagittarian; an avoider of heights; a full-licensed driver; a wearer of glasses; a person who celebrates birthdays awkwardly; a person who often (and embarrassingly) mishears; an introvert who is often very good at pretending to be an extrovert.

This is a list of broken bones; a person who sheds
a foster-related category; an often-of days-left
hardware of this person; a dinker of paper; a
wanderer of patterned tights; a frequenter of
second-hand shops; a dedicated recycler; a
frugal person; a grower of vegetables; a lazy
cook; a feeder of chickens; a polydactyl cat's
human; an omnivore; a person with size 5 feet;
a person who always has to hem their pants;
a six-toe-nailed person; a person with no
piercings; a person with an accidental tattoo;
a doodler; a feather-weight drunk; a queen
of vehicular slumber; a flirt; a dark-haired
person; a dark-eyed person; a Sagittarian;
an avoider of heights; a full-licensed driver;
a wearer of glasses; a person who celebrates
birthdays awkwardly; a person who often
(and embarrassingly) mishears; an introvert
who is often very good at pretending to be
an extrovert; a night owl; a person with no

This list is broken by a list; a person who has had a foster cat; a lover of a certain kind of paper; a collector of flight and frequencies; of started projects; a dedicated project a worker; a connoisseur of vegetables; a lover of a reference of chicken; a body close header of romance; a person with size 5 feet; a person who always has to hem their pants; a six-toe-nailed person; a person with no piercings; a person with an accidental tattoo; a doodler; a feather-weight drunk; a queen of vehicular slumber; a flirt; a dark-haired person; a dark-eyed person; a Sagittarian; an avoider of heights; a full-licensed driver; a wearer of glasses; a person who celebrates birthdays awkwardly; a person who often (and embarrassingly) mishears; an introvert who is often very good at pretending to be an extrovert; a night owl; a person with no a full-licensed driver; a wearer of glasses; a person who celebrates birthdays awkwardly; a person who often (and embarrassingly) mishears; an introvert who is often very good at pretending to be an extrovert; a night owl; a person with no

This list is written by a list-maker; a zinester; a fosterer of cats; a lover of sunny days; a left-hander; a ticklish person; a drinker of tea; a wearer of patterned tights; a frequenter of second-hand shops; a dedicated recycler; a frugal person; a grower of vegetables; a lazy cook; a feeder of chickens; a polydactyl cat's human; an omnivore; a person with size 5 feet; a person who always has to hem their pants; a six-toe-nailed person; a person with no piercings; a person with an accidental tattoo; a doodler; a feather-weight drunk; a queen of vehicular slumber; a flirt; a dark-haired person; a dark-eyed person; a Sagittarian; an avoider of heights; a full-licensed driver; a wearer of glasses; a person who celebrates birthdays awkwardly; a person who often (and embarrassingly) mishears; an introvert who is often very good at pretending to be an extrovert; a night owl; a person with no history of broken bones; a person who had a chocolate allergy; a biter of cuticles; a thrower of tantrums; a hoarder of paper; a collector of cellophane candy wrappers; a starter of projects; an abandoner of projects; a workaholic; a procrastinator; an avid reader; a terrible rememberer of things read; a closet reader of romances; a holder of hands; a comfortable skinny dipper; a sensually voiced person; an ex-lover to ██, ███, ████, ████, █████, ████, ██████, ███ and ██; a lover to █████; a heterosexual with curiosities; a cis-gendered woman; a fan of fluidity; a user of long-term contraceptives; a proficient spoon; a person withdrawing from social media; a Twitter non-entity; a voter; a person who gets asked 'where are you from?'; a person who gets asked 'where are you from, really?'; a person who ticks 'Other' for the Census ethnicity question *and capitalises the O*; a poet; a performance poet; a page poet; an occasional symposium speaker; a published author (*last edited [insert time here]*); a volunteer; a Macleans College graduate; an Elamite; an University of Auckland graduate; a publishing graduate; a worker in a capitalist economy; a freelancer; an ex-Auckland Art Gallery employee; a Penguin marketing administrator; an eldest child; a Year-of-the-Rabbit baby; a daughter; a daughter of a paediactric nurse and an environmental engineer; a sibling; an elder sister; a city shifter; an immigrant; a dual passport holder; a speaker of English and Mandarin; a person perceived as Asian; an Asian; a faux-Asian; a Taiwanese national; a New Zealand Citizen; 0211224885; 12-3132-0039509-00; 10110102033102; DG159135;1010 000003099462; 700653752601; 3083261318350465; 397973196; 83379766; an identity fractal; a person; **Ya-Wen Ho.**

TATTOOED ROCKS AT WHĀINGAROA: A PERSONAL ARCHAEOLOGY OF KNOWLEDGE THROUGH POETRY

MURRAY EDMOND

1 PROLOGUE: THE UNSETTLING

"Only interpretations"[1]—this reduction of Nietzsche's aphorism from his late notebooks serves as my starting point. Let it be my guide through what follows: the words of the German anti-philosopher whose self was drowned in his struggle with all that European expansionism born on the tide of Romanticism. A man at sea like me. In the wide Pacific sea. Te Moana nui a Kiwa.

What does one know? What do I know? What do you know? How did I come to know what I know? How do I know if what I know might qualify as knowledge?

Nietzsche also said: "In some remote corner of the sprawling universe, twinkling among the countless solar systems, there once was a star on which clever animals invented *knowledge*. That was the most arrogant, most mendacious minute in 'world history,' but it was only a minute. After nature caught its breath a little, the star froze, and the clever animals had to die."[2]

Poetry is as much a way of knowing as any other. And the Pacific is something to know about. Easily said. Easily misled. My own history, my own experience as a poet, and the idea that poetry is a form of knowledge, can be patched together to make a metaphoric life-raft of flotsam bits and jetsam pieces built as an example of how one gets knowledge, of how one gets knowledge that is both right and wrong, both useful and useless, and how one spends a lot of one's life after that sorting out if what one knows is worth knowing. While one is sorting, at the same time this "knowledge" is sorting itself into a constellation of facts and myths and memories and constructs, those "interpretations" Nietzsche spoke of, of which oneself is simply a part and in which many people participate and belong. Fragments of my night sky. Night: both a time for dreaming and a time for long hard work when everyone else is asleep.

After they have all gone to bed, one opens a book and there is a poem that has

---

1 Friedrich Nietzsche, *Writings from the Late Notebooks*, trans. Kate Sturge and ed. Rüdiger Bittner (Cambridge, UK: Cambridge UP, 2003).
2 Friedrich Nietzsche, *On Truth and Untruth: Selected Writings*, trans. Taylor Carman (New York: Harper, 2010), 17.

been dedicated to oneself. A poem from poet to poet. One might dedicate a poem for purposes of seduction (Sappho to Gongyla) or ridicule of an opponent (Allen Curnow's "Dichtung und Wahrheit" addressed to an unnamed M.K. Joseph) but poets also dedicate poems to other poets as if some exchange of knowledge takes place in that instance, an exchange subsumed in recent times under the aegis of "inter-textuality."

It is an unsettling thing to confront one's own name as dedicatee of a poem. In *Brief* magazine, issue 47, Scott Hamilton published a set of seven poems dedicated to me. One looks at oneself in that instance of dedication as if one were to go home of an evening and just as one is poised to slide the key into the lock, the door opens and there, standing before one, is oneself. Suddenly not one but two. The horror of the double, that staple of German Romanticism, the abyss staring back, bestows an unsettling shift of being.

You wonder about yourself. Who is that with that name written there? What does this poet know about that person? What exchange have I been involved in without my knowing?

Here is the first of Scott Hamilton's poems:

"An Apology for the Revival of Christian Architecture in Hamilton East"

That iron cross is also a weathervane.
Once you saw it trembling reverently
In a storm.

All that night your bed floated towards Valparaiso.
You shut your eyes
And watched the lightning flash on and off
Like a buoy in a heavy break.

You imagined angels convulsing
On their black cloud-beds,
And depressives getting their ration of ECT
Over the hill at Tokanui.[3]

This poem is dedicated to me and I think that this is because it is about my home town in Aotearoa: Hamilton, the place where I grew up.

---

3 Scott Hamilton, "Seven Urban Legends (for Murray Edmond)," *Brief* 47 (March 2013): 95.

2 SETTLEMENT

Perhaps Scott knew that as a boy I attended St Andrew's Presbyterian Church, which is across the Waikato River on the eastern bank of the town, in Hamilton East. There is certainly a church in the poem.

The next thing to appear in the poem is the city of Valparaiso, 9,500 kilometres to the east, almost on the same latitude as Hamilton. The poem depicts Valparaiso as a place of the night, as a dream place—"your bed floated towards Valparaiso." So why did Scott choose to include that distant city of Valparaiso? The reason is that Scott has knowledge of my poetry, particularly a poem called "Von Tempsky's Dance" that was written in 1971:

> where the feet of the mind
> dance, quitting to Valparaiso, Santiago,[4]

I included Valparaiso in the poem because to reach it in my imagination meant stretching out a line far to the east, across that vast stretch of water, to the eastern edge of the Pacific. Aotearoa/New Zealand was colonized by people from Europe, my ancestors among them, but its place is in the Pacific, the Great Ocean of Kiwa. The poem says: "on that island [Rapa Nui / Easter Island], in South Chile too, / The gold sophora grows. The voice too / is indigenous as it walks about / where it is."[5] The gold Sophora is the Kowhai tree, with its golden flowers in spring, famous in the title *Kowhai Gold*, the first anthology of New Zealand poetry published in the 1920s. In the "Von Tempsky" poem (1971), written shortly after my "escape" from Hamilton (1968) to study at Auckland University, I was trying to locate myself, in both psychic and geographic senses, in the Pacific. And in locating myself I was trying to pit myself against the nineteenth century historical figure of Gustavus Ferdinand Von Tempsky: "my voice sends itself & yearns / dangling on Von Tempsky's hilt."[6] I imagine my voice having been run through by Von Tempsky's sword.

Gustavus Von Tempsky came from Prussia and was of Polish ancestry. He had spent time in California and the Mosquito Coast of Central America. He is most remembered in New Zealand for his role fighting as a kind of mercenary, with his own little company called The Forest Rangers, in the Government forces against Māori during a portion of the period of the land wars, the years from 1863 to 1868. He was killed in 1868 at the battle of Te Ngutu o te Manu in Taranaki. Von Tempsky also fought in the Waikato, which is both the iwi name, Waikato, and also the area

---

4   Murray Edmond, "Von Tempsky's Dance," in *The Penguin Book of New Zealand Verse*, eds. Ian Wedde and Harvey McQueen (Auckland: Penguin, 1985), 504.

5   Edmond, "Von Tempsky's Dance," 504.

6   Edmond, "Von Tempsky's Dance," 505.

name for the place where the city of Hamilton sits astride the Waikato River. Von Tempsky fought at the Battle of Orakau and was, according to Wikipedia, "heavily implicated in the massacre that followed the breakout of the defenders."[7] Do we believe Wikipedia? Does Wikipedia supply true knowledge? In the New Zealand on-line encyclopedia known as Te Ara, the new biography of Von Tempsky provides a more ambiguous account of that battle: "When the defenders broke out of the pa at Orakau, he [Von Tempsky] led his men in a ruthless pursuit but strongly disapproved when the British troops killed some of the wounded and women. He encouraged his men to intervene to prevent these atrocities."[8] Instinctively we know that the truth about war is probably always worse and less heroic than the stories that are told. So, in this case, which story about Von Tempsky is true? Was he a kind of romantic outlier adventurer in the story of the colonization of Aotearoa or was he a mercenary with the blood of a massacre on his hands? I think it was the ambiguous nature of Von Tempsky as a character from history—not a good guy undoubtedly, but one who earned his own appellation from Māori as "Manurau" or "one hundred birds," in other words, the man who is everywhere—that attracted me to write the poem about him, when I was 21 years old. At the time I was living in a student flat in Grafton Road in Auckland, number 60 Grafton Road, and two doors away, at number 64, Von Tempsky had lived briefly in the 1860s in a cottage that still stood and still (2016) stands there. I was working on a sequence of poems I called "The Grafton Notebook" and the impetus for writing "Von Tempsky's Dance" had come from my neighbor, Ngahuia Te Awekotuku (then Ngahuia Volkering), who lived at 56 Grafton Road. One day Ngahuia had said to me, "My nightmare is that one day I'll see him [Von Tempsky] come riding down the gully":

In No.64 Von Tempsky has his picture up
I am uncertain where he lived
I am uncertain where he lives
& he is out of breath
& out for blood
in a dance that that yearns to know
how old, how far, & when & where to go.[9]

After the Battle of Orakau the Waikato iwi withdrew from fighting behind a line drawn at the Waipa and Puniu Rivers into a fastness called in English "The

7 "Gustvaus von Tempsky," accessed September 14, 2016, https://en.wikipedia.org/wiki/Gustavus_von_Tempsky.
8 N.A.C. McMillan, "Story: Tempsky, Gustavus Ferdinand von," accessed September 14, 2016, http://www.teara.govt.nz/en/biographies/1t90/tempsky-gustavus-ferdinand-von.
9 Edmond, "VonTempsky's Dance," 504.

King Country" (after Tawhiao the second Māori King) or in Māori Te Rohe Pōtae, literally "the rim of the hat." Māori became excluded from the mainstream of economic life in the Waikato and in many ways lived a separate existence, almost like a country within a country, which most Pākehā were not aware of. The ancestral lands had been lost in fighting; and they were then confiscated by the Government as punishment for "rebellion." Some of this land was parceled to soldiers as "rewards" or payment for services; Von Tempsky received a grant of land near Mount Pirongia, but never took it up because he was killed in the fighting in Taranaki. And it was on these confiscated lands that the town of Hamilton was built at a place known already as Kirikiriroa (referring to the sandbanks at that point in the Waikato River). Hamilton's connection to the war was reinforced by being named after an officer killed in the Battle of Gate Pa near Tauranga. Most of the soldiers looked at the largely swampy terrain now known as Hamilton and left for Australia. One, a surveyor and painter, Captain Charles Heaphy, laid out the street plan for the new town: Boundary Road (the edge of the city) and of course Heaphy Terrace. I rode along these roads on my bike to high school when I was growing up in Hamilton in the 1960s, but I did not know, nor inquire about, and no one told me, the stories that lay behind these names. My friends Angela and Felicity Day lived on Von Tempsky Street. Writing a poem about Von Tempsky became for me a step towards knowing about the place where I had grown up, a "step," perhaps in the sense a dancer might use the word. Nietzsche: "I wouldn't know what the spirit of a philosopher might more want to be than a good dancer."[10]

After Hamilton and Valparaiso, Scott's poem takes us to a third place, Tokanui, meaning literally in Māori "the big boulder / the big rock"; Tokanui was the psychiatric hospital for the Waikato. The name was used as a synonym for "crazy" when I was growing up in Hamilton. "Don't be tokanui" we would say, meaning "Don't be stupid." It was there, in Tokanui Hospital, that the so-called "mad" received "their ration of ECT" (electro-convulsive therapy, a treatment widely used in New Zealand during the 1950s, 1960s and into the 1970s and beyond). There was great fear of mental hospitals in the 1950s and 1960s. There were over 1,000 patients living in Tokanui during those years, but they were shut away from sight and we borrowed the name of their home as a word of abuse.

What had happened in the Waikato over the century from 1864 to 1964 was a process called "settlement." Settlement implies both moving into an area and taking it over, as Pākehā did, and also "settling down" or "coming to rest." The Hamilton I grew up in during the 1950s and 1960s was a place that had "come to rest"—or so it seemed to me. It was a rural service town supporting the values of farming (Pākehā farmers with dairy herds and fat lambs) and soldiering (most of the men, who would

---

10 Friedrich Nietzsche, *The Gay Science*, trans. Josefine Nauckhoff (Cambridge: Cambridge University Press, 2001), 246.

come to run the town, had not long since returned from the Second World War) and rugby (whereby men assuaged a certain loneliness). People not attached to these core values were slightly suspicious, perhaps even "tokanui." My father, a returned soldier from the war, sold cars to the rich farmers, and we played rugby on Saturdays and went to church on Sundays. We were part of the "settlement." This settlement is characterized by Kendrick Smithyman, in his poem "Waikato Railstop," through the image of "flight" (or lack of it):

> There was also
> an engineer who built an aircraft in his backyard,
> which he could not fly; ambition was not licensed
> to go soaring. Such an ascent measures most days'
> custom of being flat.[11]

3 DON'T DREAM IT BE IT

What if you and your girlfriend/boyfriend were to drive out from Hamilton into the countryside, say beyond Ohaupo, one dark and stormy night, and your car were to break down and, looking about for assistance, you spied a strange and interesting looking house where you might get help and you knocked on the front door of that house. . . and a hunchback butler named Riff Raff opened the door and greeted you, and in that house it turned out there lived a bunch of aliens who wanted nothing more than to bring you sexual pleasure and musical joy by playing rock 'n' roll? This was not quite what the "settlers" of Hamilton had in mind when they took the land. But it was certainly on the mind of Richard O'Brien when he worked in the barber's shop by the Embassy Theatre in Victoria Street, the main street of Hamilton, in the years 1959–1964, over the time I was finishing primary school and starting high school. When he came to write his musical *The Rocky Horror Show*, in Shepherd's Bush in London, he said he had met all the characters in the streets of Hamilton. So, yes, I am suggesting that we can read *The Rocky Horror Show*, with its message of "Don't dream it, be it," as a show about growing up in the Waikato in mid-twentieth century, and that in terms of the knowledge that can be found in poetry, these words bring knowledge of that place:

> In the velvet darkness
> Of the blackest night

---

11 Kendrick Smithyman, "Waikato Railstop," in *Selected Poems*, ed. Peter Simpson (Auckland: Auckland University Press, 1989), 55.

Burning bright - there's a guiding star
No matter what or who you are
There's a light
Over at the Frankenstein place
There's a light[12]

O'Brien's song includes rather than excludes; it says that the light is there for everyone "No matter what or who you are," and therefore stands in opposition to the settled world of farming and soldiering and rugby. At the same time as being inclusive, the song, in the best revivalist traditions, is an invitation to escape, to follow that "guiding star" to "the Frankenstein place." Escape is a theme of the literature of the Waikato, an implied impossibility in the image of Smithyman's engineer who could not fly the plane he built, and realized in actuality by the creation of the haven of Te Rohe Potae after Orakau. Escape *into* the Waikato is a rarer thing, but it is there in one of the foundational literary texts of the Waikato, William Satchell's *The Greenstone Door*. Purcell, the Pākehā-Māori figure of that novel, who is "as deeply clothed in mystery as that of the Man in the Iron Mask," has chosen to abandon his "civilized" white world for "the arms of savagery" and never shows any "regret for the life he had left behind him."[13] Purcell's adopted son, Cedric, comments upon leaving the Waikato and arriving in Auckland for the first time: "If this were civilization, then give me savagery."[14]

Victoria Street now boasts a statue of Richard O'Brien, captured in bronze as Riff-Raff, Frank-n-Furter's butler: "Everything is in readiness master."[15] The plinth below the statue tells us that here O'Brien "cut hair and daydreamed." Where the statue stands now, the demolished Embassy Theatre once stood. In *The Rocky Horror Picture Show* O'Brien's own romance was with the movies, the "flicks" as they were called then; but for Brad and Janet, the naïve hero and heroine in his high camp rock 'n' roll musical, their romance is less with each other than with experiential self-discovery. For Brad and Janet the drama stages an education in pleasure fed by forbidden fruit: "Don't dream it—Be it."[16] Hamilton is now probably seven times bigger than it was in O'Brien's (and my) time. Yet still the frontages of the shops where Riff-Raff stands retain something of the setting of the white colonial frontier town of 1864, the settler town: like facades from a Western movie, just two stories high with false fronts. In 2009 I went there and made an inventory of the shops beside the O'Brien statue: one, garishly decorated,

---

12 Richard O'Brien, *The Rocky Horror Show*, (London: Samuel French, 1983), 6.
13 William Satchell, *The Greenstone Door* (Auckland: Golden Press, 1980 [1914]), 41.
14 Satchell, *Greenstone Door*, 125.
15 O'Brien, *Rocky Horror*, 12.
16 O'Brien, *Rocky Horror*, 29.

advertised a secondhand-clothes shop called "Madam Muck"; another was a down-at-heel sex shop from which half the sign had fallen, proffering "pecialities [sic] lingerie novelties or pleasure"; a third sign soberly announced "New Zealand Arts & Gifts" though the shop was closed. One is reminded of John Lennon's famous reply, when asked how he found New Zealand: "It was closed."

4 THE TATTOOED ROCKS

Like O'Brien, I too dreamed that there was a place where you could *be*—beyond the false facades of main street, beyond the suburban lake of little houses, the clusters of shops, beyond the fat green pastures of butter and cream, beyond the land wrested as confiscations, which has paid back the military investment many-fold. My dream was not of rock 'n' roll aliens, but of the world of the bush and the seashore, of what outside "the generally depauperate natural environment of Hamilton"[17] (as Rufus Wells put it) remained of the land that had not been turned into farms that were really factories. I was swept off my feet by that tall, dark stranger, knowledge, in the form of the idea that there were other, richer and more complex worlds to be found through science. I was 11 years old, in Form One, when Pat Devlin came to our classroom at Vardon School and spoke to us about the naturalist club he was going to start:

> I was a young itinerant science adviser with 110 schools in the South Auckland Education Board. It was 1961 . . . . During visits to schools . . . . I would usually spend some time talking to [the] class, introducing a topic from the syllabus, reviewing work . . . conducting fieldwork—whatever it took to extend and sometimes excite the children and, through them, the teacher. It was during these encounters that I would find one or two children in a class who would ask or answer most of the questions, whose eyes were bright and whose attention was undivided.[18]

I became one of these bright-eyed children. Pat's enthusiastic vision captured my imagination, and I signed up to the Hamilton Junior Naturalists Club and began to attend the weekly meetings held on Friday evenings, initially in the original Teachers' Training College in Melville, then in Peachgrove Intermediate School. The meetings were our theory occasions where visiting speakers or Pat himself talked on some topic, and we organised field trips for the weekends, trips

---

17 Rufus Wells, "An Unnatural History," *Landfall* 180 (Dec. 1991): 422.
18 Pat Devlin, "Junats: young boots in the bush," *NZ Science Teacher* 108 (2005): 9.

where we went to the bush or the seashore armed with our notebooks for recording what we found. I still think of the time I spent at the club (1961–1966) as one of my best educational experiences, a balanced and creative combination of theory and practice.

On 7 October 1961 we went on a field trip to Raglan. Raglan, or Whāingaroa (its other name I did not know then), is a large shallow harbour 40 kilometres to the west of Hamilton. We went there to study the bush and stream life and also, as my field notes record, "the seashore life in the different tidal zones." My trip report continued, "The tide was out so every zone could be observed." I came home to Hamilton with some knowledge of the structure of rocky-shore ecology. A diagram in my field report lists plants and animals in four zones: the Splash Zone, the High Tide Zone, the Mid-Tide Zone, and the Low Tide Zone. This idea of zonation received its articulation from Lucy M. Cranwell in her 1938 article "Intertidal communities of the Poor Knights Islands, New Zealand." Cranwell went on to pioneer the field of palynology in the USA. Along with her fellow botanical Lucy, Lucy Moore, she formed the founding duo of modern botany in New Zealand. After H.H. Allan's death, Moore completed Allan's work on *The Flora of New Zealand* (1961), and this treasured book (there were further volumes to come), with tissue-thin pages, we carried in our naturalist rucksacks. One afternoon as we wended our way along the Oparau Road on the southern slopes of Mount Pirongia, a car drew up beside our straggling band of Junior Naturalists, and sitting in the car was the famous figure of Dr. Moore. We felt the gods had visited. My Raglan field trip report records the words "Echinoderms, Molluscs, Crustaceans and Coelenterates." I was finding a new vocabulary to describe the world, acquiring an ability to see and to distinguish that I did not have before—and also discovering something of the poetry of science. Our reports were handed in to Pat Devlin for marking the Friday following the trip. The "Junats" club felt more *serious* than school, certainly more exciting.

At the same time as I was discovering the language of the natural sciences, as they were called then, I was beginning to make attempts to write poetry— palimpsest versions of nonsense poems my father recited on trips in the car or of pieces from Palgrave's *The Golden Treasury of the Best Poems and Songs in the English Language*. The year was 1961, but my tiny knowledge of poetry was from the mid-nineteenth century, "Victorian," like the name of the main street of Hamilton. One populist book on New Zealand flora, *The Plants of New Zealand*, by R.M. Laing, and E.W. Blackwell, included Victorian poetry in small dollops throughout its text: the transcendentalist American Emerson, for example, but also nineteenth century New Zealand bards such as David McKee Wright, Alfred Domett, and William Pember Reeves. Laing and Blackwell's book had first been published by Whitcombe and Tombs in 1907, when much of this poetry had been almost contemporary. I possessed the sixth edition published in 1957, and by that time the poetry was distinctly archaic. The "General Introduction" spoke of the vanished world of the bush in a tone that was elegiac and nostalgic: "Whatever may have been the causes in the past, affecting the reduction or increase of forest areas, they fall into insignificance compared with the changes artificially wrought since the arrival of Europeans."[19] This commentary was rounded out by a large chunk of the text of William Pember Reeves' poem "The Passing of the Forest." Reeves was a significant politician, a kind of progressive Fabian socialist, but also the author of the Undesirable Immigrants Exclusion Bill, which was aimed at excluding Asian immigrants and the poor from the deforested paradise of Aotearoa. The poem evokes both the theory of evolution—"Creeper with creeper, bush with bush at strife," the idea of the survival of the fittest—and a lament for what has been lost— "Gone are the forest tracks where oft we rode / Under the silvery fern fronds"[20]—as if Reeves wants to have his land and eat it too, so to speak. Reeves' poem tries to combine poetry and science and I was trying to do the same thing in my own small way in 1961. Looking back I think the result was both an ordering and a disordering of world and language that may be common in a first encounter with new knowledge. How to combine poetry and science was a question paralleled by the question of how to combine a "settled" picture of the world, such as my Hamilton childhood presented, with new knowledge about the world that I did not know how to verify or process. That poetry is a kind of knowledge is an idea one must learn, as it were, "against" much of what one is taught. Contrary to the dubious truths of poetry, science as knowledge lays claim to a myth (in Roland Barthes' sense) about its irrefutable truth that pervades our modern world. And the Hamilton Junior Naturalists was a scientific club in its aspirations, desiring that "ascent" of truth that would overcome the "custom of being flat."

My field report from the 1961 Raglan trip records another discovery made that day: "An interesting find . . . was the tattooed rock. This rock is a large rock situated at the top of the splash zone. It is covered with black curly tattoo marks. It is thought that some sailor landed before Abel Tasman and tattooed the rock with tar. The tar ate into the rock and so left it tattooed forever. The tattooings are thought to be of Arabic origin." My account of the rock is accompanied with a clumsy crayon and pencil drawing, showing what are clearly koru patterns, and therefore certainly not Arabic, but Māori, as even the popular nomenclature of "Tattooed Rocks" acknowledged implicitly. However someone in our "scientific" club had told us they were Arabic, and I had dutifully written it down. It seems I was not the only one reaching for something "beyond the settlement," but that here was an example of "over-reaching." In a short article in the *Journal of the Polynesian Society* in

---

19 R.M. Laing and E.W. Blackwell, *The Plants of New Zealand* (Christchurch: Whitcombe and Tombs, 1957), 12–13.

20 Laing and Blackwell, *Plants*, 14.

reference to one of the designs, W. J. Phillipps comments: "we have already noted this type of head from Taranaki" and the appearance of "manaia'" and "koru" are mentioned among the tattooings.[21]

The rock I saw has been an object of enduring fascination, along with other similar rocks, and other objects from the same coastline, sometimes involving speculations of the "Arabic" kind, which I have followed up in an attempt to understand where this fabrication came from. Phillipps' article mentions "some twelve stones . . . inscribed at one time or another."[22] C.G. Hunt in an account compiled for the Waikato Scientific Society in 1955, *Some Notes on the Mystery Wreck on Ruapuke Beach*, stated that it was thought "among old settlers at Raglan" that "there were four of these rocks."[23] Hunt went hunting himself and found two rocks; I saw only one, though we always referred to them as the tattooed rocks, as if there were more than one. Hunt's article discusses (though does not endorse) the connections that have been made between the wreck of a ship, which had been exposed from time to time on Ruapuke Beach, south of Whāingaroa/Raglan, and the Tattooed Rocks. The rock, which I saw, is situated at Manu Bay just south of the main ocean beach at Raglan. Hunt outlines the connections that had been made among the mystery objects from the area: the wreck was that "of a Tamil ship and its bell was in existence" and the ship "pre-dated the arrival of Captain Cook" and the "graves near the wreck were those of victims of the disaster" and "the patterns on the 'Tattooed Rocks' had been done by the survivors." These notions tied in with what I had been told as an 11-year-old. That is not the end of the bundling of curiosities and fabricated mysteries, for Hunt adds three more pearls to the string: "that the stone columns in nearby Māori pas showed an outside influence on local Māori customs," "that the Korotangi [a smallish statue of a bird of unknown origin] was brought to New Zealand on this vessel," and "that the wreck is so old that modern Māoris have no legends about it."[24] Somewhere along the line "Arabic" had been substituted for "Tamil" in the account I received on that field trip. It is apparent these kinds of speculations had leaked into what was and still is a club determinedly devoted to science. But the history of such speculation is long and deep within the Pākehā imagination confronted with the reality of the Māori settlement of Aotearoa. I was picking up a tradition of pseudo-knowledge that stretched back, like the poems in Laing and Blackwell, into the nineteenth century.

Kerry Howe is the historian who has dealt with (and *to*) the persistent desire

---

21 W.J. Phillipps, "Incised Rocks, Raglan," *Journal of the Polynesian Society* 71, no. 4 (Dec. 1962): 402.
22 Phillipps, "Incised Rocks": 400.
23 C.G. Hunt, *Some Notes on the Mystery Wreck on Ruapuke Beach* (Hamilton: Waikato Scientific Association, 1955), 36.
24 Hunt, *Mystery Wreck*, 1.

to find Polynesian origins amongst "the Greeks, Egyptians, Phoenicians, Libyans, Minoans, Mesopotamians."[25] Howe, in the article quoted above, points up the Euro-centric and imperialist origin of such thinking, as well as its connections with the new developments in sciences such as archaeology, anthropology, and geology during the nineteenth century. Even Māori scholar Peter Buck/Te Rangi Hiroa argued that Māori "may have originated in the Middle East and 'probably did live in some part of India.'"[26] Such ideas were very likely the source of "Arabic" being ascribed to the tattooed rock.

Another persistent pseudo-scientific myth was the idea that the arrival of Māori was an "invasion" which swept aside a pre-Māori people (then Moriori, now Waitaha) who already occupied Aotearoa, usually in a peaceful and "spiritual" manner, as opposed to warlike Māori. It is hard not to hear in this story the wish-fulfillment of the Pākehā colonizer—they did it, so we can do it too—as well as the whisper of the progressivism of Social Darwinism. And I was able to find this idea of a pre-Māori settlement tucked away in my write-up of a "Field Trip to the Aotea Harbour Area" on 5 October 1963 (Aotea is another big shallow harbour not far south of the tattooed rocks and the shipwreck and north of the place where the Korotangi is reputed to have been found) which describes an "archaelogical site"—"a small, low, and dusty cave in the side of a dry hillside" and labels this as "pre-Māori" consisting of "shell diggings . . . up to 6ft. deep at the back." Another example of the romantic fabrication of knowledge is the intrusion of mysterious visitors evidenced by such things as "ancient shipwrecks on New Zealand's wild west coast beaches that are reputed to be uncovered briefly in storms"[27]—like the one on Ruapuke Beach which Hunt investigates. It is to C.G. Hunt's credit, writing as he is in 1955, that he comments: "At times I was amazed at the fantastic theories which had been woven round the flimsiest of evidence."[28] As Howe points out with regard to the Korotangi carving of a bird (made of serpentine and clearly not Polynesian) that "it is even possible that it is as banal an object as an Italian garden ornament brought to New Zealand in nineteenth-century colonial baggage."[29] The likely truth about the graves exposed in sand hills at Ruapuke Beach, near the wreck, is both poignant and also historically more telling than some more fantastic explanation. They are almost certainly early twentieth-century hasty burials of Māori who died in an epidemic, possibly the 1919 influenza epidemic: "The deaths

25 Kerry Howe, "Māori/Polynesian Origins and 'The New Learning'," *Journal of the Polynesian Society* 108 (1999): 306.
26 Kerry Howe, *The Quest for Origins: Who First Discovered and Settled New Zealand and the Pacific Islands* (Auckland: Penguin, 2003), 172.
27 Howe, *Quest*, 145.
28 Hunt, *Mystery Wreck*, 1.
29 Howe, *Quest*, 145.

had been numerous and the burials difficult to cope with so the dead had been buried in hastily made coffins in the sand-hills."[30] Hunt's investigations finally turned up an admission from a local farmer, William Thomson, about the time of the exposure of the coffins in 1946–48: "When a reporter arrived to investigate, some of the local wits had decided to play a practical joke on him and had spread wild rumours of seven-foot skeletons in the coffins, fair hair and conjectures that the skeletons were those of the victims of the wreck which had been a Viking ship. Much of this had appeared in the press."[31] Similar rumours also appeared in my field trip notebook, in the disguise of knowledge.

In 1966 I went on my last Junior Naturalists field trip, to Mayor Island/Tuhua off the Bay of Plenty coast. Obsidian from Mayor Island would later be found on an archaeological dig on Raoul Island in the Kermadecs at a site dated to the thirteenth century. Atholl Anderson reads this extraordinary discovery not as evidence of return voyaging by Māori, but as explorative voyaging in what he calls "South Polynesia" by those recent arrivals in Aotearoa who were to become Māori.[32] He links sites of precarious and impermanent settlement from Norfolk Island, the Chathams, the Auckland Islands and possibly even Australia, which have been dated contemporaneously with the Raoul Island site to create an extraordinary picture of restless, explorative voyaging.

I was now 16, not 11 anymore, staying on Mayor Island for a week, as restless as a thirteenth-century Polynesian voyager. My relationship with the club came apart with a disagreement about poetry. Someone had brought to the camp the words and tune of a song called "Plastic Jesus." Paul Newman sang it a year later as part of his masterly performance in the film *Cool Hand Luke* (1967). The plastic Jesus in the song is a modern American effigy or totem, which rides on the dashboard of a New York taxi:

I don't care if it rains or freezes.
Long as I got my plastic Jesus.

The little god figure has a sacramental secret:

For His head comes off, you see
He's hollow, and I use him for a flask.

---

30 Hunt, *Mystery Wreck*, 8.
31 Hunt, *Mystery Wreck*, 8.
32 Atholl Anderson, "Retrievable Time: prehistoric colonization of South Polynesia from the outside in and the inside out," in *Disputed Histories: Imagining New Zealand's Pasts*, eds. Tony Ballantyne and Brian Moloughney (Dunedin: Otago University Press, 2006), 25.

So in the evenings we sang together to a guitar:

> Ride with me and have a dram
> Of the blood of the Lamb
> Plastic Jesus is a holy bar.[33]

While some of us at least were more than ready to applaud the sacrilegious sentiments of the song, it was understandably too much for club supervisor Pat Devlin and we were forbidden to sing the song. We had reached one of those gateways in knowledge where something needs to shift for the teacher/student relationship to continue. Obnoxious teenagers we undoubtedly were, but also we were growing up and the hypocrisy and pomposity of the world was begging to be pricked with a pin: "The surest way to corrupt a youth is to instruct him to hold in higher esteem those who think alike than those who think differently."[34]

5 GHOSTS OF KNOWLEDGE

The persistence of fantastical stories has typically been interwoven with evidence-based scientific enquiry. Howe quotes Glyn Daniel about the "general romance" of archaeology and also points to the politics of these ideas and the way they are bound up with "both colonialist and anti-colonialist ideology."[35] The venture of the Naturalists' Club had some features picked up from nineteenth-century imperialist and Euro-centric ideas. In my own growing up these ideas sometimes became confused with the more progressive desire to move beyond the "settled" world of Hamilton. In its progressive aspect, the club opened my mind to the natural world of Aotearoa/New Zealand, which, along with Māori society, had borne the brunt of "settlement." "Natural world" is a phrase that sits awkwardly because it means no more than what one wants it to mean—and yet in Aotearoa, because it is one of the last settled places on earth (other islands of Polynesia are "ancient" in comparison, though Rapa-nui, for example, may have a similar settlement date), we can still easily find places without any evidence of human presence cheek-by-jowl with places whose "naturalness" has been wiped from the face of the landscape in a very short space of time.

There is always a politics of knowledge, as there is a politics of romance, as Brad and Janet find with Frank-n-Furter, as Frank-n-Furter discovers with Rocky in *The Rocky Horror Picture Show*. That which starts out with bright eyes and

---

33 "Plastic Jesus," accessed September 14, 2016, http://www.guntheranderson.com/v/data/plastic0.htm.
34 Friedrich Nietzsche, *The Dawn of Day*, trans. J. M. Kennedy (London: T.N. Foulis, 1911).
35 Howe, *Quest*, 158.

undivided attention later has to re-think its understanding or justify its position. Knowledge is not static. The reverse also happens: the erection of the Riff-Raff statue is a recuperation of knowledge, an inclusion of what was once excluded. The Riff-Raff statue is there now in the main street, though Queen Victoria may not be amused if she were to find out. And the hospital at Tokanui closed in 1998, as ideas about how to care for and treat people suffering from mental disturbance changed. The archaeological metaphor would speak of an artifact disappearing under accumulations of detritus or of an old object long buried suddenly exposed by the wind and water action, like those coffins in the sand hills.

Recuperations of knowledge also happen in poetry. When I decided to write about the Tattooed Rocks, I went looking for a poem in so-called New Zealand Literature (a term a little like "natural world") that mentioned Whāingaroa/Raglan. I found that mention in Te Puea Hērangi's waiata, "E Noho, e Rata," in the 1985 *Penguin Book of New Zealand Verse*, the anthology edited by Ian Wedde and Harvey McQueen which challenged the earlier 1960 *Penguin Anthology* of Allen Curnow's in its inclusion of modern Māori language waiata/poetry, giving the poetry of Aotearoa/ New Zealand a heritage in two languages. (Curnow had included pre-European Māori waiata of various kinds.) This was an act of poetic recuperation because New Zealand Poetry must always have been in two languages (at least), but this reality had been avoided up until the Wedde/McQueen anthology appeared. Te Puea Hērangi (better known as Princess Te Puea) composed the song "E Noho, E Rata" in 1917, at the time she was opposing Māori soldiers going to the First World War. Rata was then the fourth of the Māori Kings since the Kingship/Kīngitanga had been created in 1858 as a major political organizational step in the resistance to the settlement of the Waikato that came to an end in military terms only with the defeat at Orakau. However the Kīngitanga did not disappear. It emerged from the King Country (Te Rohe Pōtae) in 1883 and re-inhabited what "tongi" (spots) of land remained. In this waiata, which has become like a national anthem of the King Movement, Te Puea guides Rata on a tour of the tribal territory of his people, including to where the Tattooed Rocks lie, at Raglan/Whāingaroa beneath Karioi mountain:

Tō pikitanga ko te ao o te rangi,
Tō heketanga ko Karioi maunga,
Tō hoenga-ā-waka ko Whāingaroa,

You will mount up on the clouds of the sky,
You will go down at Mount Karioi!
Your paddling place is Whāingaroa,[36]

---

36 Te Puea Hērangi, "E Noho, E Rata," trans. Margaret Orbell, in *The Penguin Book of New Zealand Verse*, eds. Ian Wedde and Harvey McQueen (Auckland: Penguin, 1985), 133–134.

At the end of her tour in the waiata Te Puea comes to Ngāruawahia, "ki Ngāruawaahia," which she describes as "Tūrangawaewae o te Kīngitanga," foothold of the Kingitanga. This part of the waiata takes a prophecy made by Tāwhiao, the second Māori King, that Ngāruawaahia, 20 kilometeres north of Hamilton on the Waikato River, would become the centre of the Kīngitanga; it was there during the 1930s that Te Puea guided the building of the marae of Tūrangawaewae on swampy land on the edge of the Waikato River in a place that had recently been used as a rubbish dump. Such a marae, both new in that it was not built on an ancestral site and old in that it became the focal marae for the Kīngitanga, began to redraw the map of the Waikato. It was not the kind of place Charles Heaphy had included in his survey of Hamilton in 1964.

Those, such as Heaphy, who made maps to envision the future were also those who did not want to know that their vision of the future might not turn out. Those maps were as much part of a desire to escape the place they were in as was my desire to escape from the stifling world of Hamilton in the1960s. Escape is a colonial condition. William Satchell pinpoints the nature of this desire in *The Greenstone Door*: "untrained and undisciplined white men; the majority of whom, moreover, had not developed any affection for the country, and merely desired to make money rapidly in order that they might leave it."[37] Satchell catches the paradox of the colonial project, that colonists want to grab the land so that they might "leave" it. The urge to escape that often had driven people out of their own country attached itself permanently once the colonial enterprise began. Amnesia is often acknowledged as part of the colonial condition, but escape also characterizes it, the desire not only to forget, but also not to know.

Robin Hyde tagged this desire onto Charles Heaphy in her poem "Young Knowledge." The appearance of this poem in the 1985 Wedde/McQueen anthology was another act of recuperation. "Young Knowledge" had been published in Hyde's posthumous 1953 volume *Houses By the Sea* but had not been picked up by earlier anthologists. "Young Knowledge," a poem about knowledge, is a substantial (147 lines), rich and puzzling poem. It may even be two poems (or more) conflated in posthumous publication. Heaphy makes a late entry into the poem at line 133. His entry is heralded by Hyde's necromantic evocation of knowledge:

And these I know, and ghosts of dead men's knowledge,
(And ghosts of young, rebellious, chidden knowledge,
Dunce at its class and striding out of school)
By bridges slender as the aka ladder
Where Heaphy, climbing, found the Greenstone People,
Saw the wide nets wash out in thundering surf

---

37 Satchell, *Greenstone Door*, 203.

Too huge for the canoes, drawn in by moonlight;
Watched the brown women drying out inanga
For fodder in the nights of eaten moons[38]

These lines convey well the densely woven verbal texture of the poem; their sometimes disconnected syntax line to line makes one wonder about which part might have been meant to be joined to which part. Hyde's poem draws on a passage in Heaphy's journal of his journey in 1846 down the West Coast of the South Island "looking for natural resources and arable land on behalf of the New Zealand Company,"[39] which describes the small Māori community he stumbled on at Arahura:

> We found here about six men and fifteen women, with a large proportion of children. The inmates of each house were busily engaged in making *meri poenamu* [greenstone adzes] and ear pendants of that material for 'trade' or presents to the northward. They saw the slab with a piece of mica slate, wet, and afterwards polish it with a fine sandy limestone which they obtain in the vicinity. The hole is drilled with a stick pointed with a piece of Pahutani flint . . . . They fish in the shallow parts of the Teremakau and Mawhera rivers in the summer, catching eels, soles, and whitebait . . . . There are no canoes large enough to proceed to sea . . . . It is probably the worst off community in New Zealand.[40]

"Young Knowledge" winds up to its conclusion:

> When wind prowls round the thatch with thievish fingers;
> Saw the marled greenstone littered on the ground,
> And how they fine the edge with whalebone drills -
> And standing on the clifftops, saw their smokes
> Final stream up, blue parting of a dream.
> There standing on the clifftops weighed his knowledge -
> The thin precarious weight of early knowledge -
> And staring in a sun, half steeled his heart
> To tell the cities there was no such world.[41]

---

38 Robin Hyde, "Young Knowledge," in *Young Knowledge: The Poems of Robin Hyde*, ed. Michele Leggott (Auckland: Auckland University Press, 2003), 206–207.

39 Michele Leggott, "Introduction," in *Young Knowledge: The Poems of Robin Hyde* (Auckland: Auckland University Press, 2003), 1.

40 Charles Heaphy, "Notes of an Expedition to Kawatiri and Araura on the Western Coast of the Middle island," in *Early Travellers in New Zealand*, ed. Nancy M. Taylor (Oxford: Clarendon Press, 1959), 237–238.

41 Hyde, "Young Knowledge," 207.

Hyde imagines Heaphy making a political decision about knowledge: as he looks on something utterly separate, strange and alien from him ("blue parting of a dream"), he decides to turn away and deny the existence of what he has seen: "To tell the cities there was no such world." As Hyde's editor Michele Leggott notes, the expedition did not find "the broad river plains reported by Māori and urgently needed by the farmers of the Nelson settlement."[42] Heaphy was on official watch for exactly what Satchell names—land from which they "desired to make money rapidly in order that they might leave it."

Charles Heaphy, the man who, in his role as Chief Surveyor to the Central Government (January 1864 to December 1865), surveyed the confiscated land in the Waikato for the new military settlements of Hamilton and Cambridge, was the epitome of the colonial optimist (one who takes and escapes), an adventurer (but not in Von Tempsky's sense) and jack-of-all-trades all his life. A member of the Royal Academy at age 17, he sailed to New Zealand in 1839 as Artist and Surveyor for the New Zealand Company, a venture in colonization as business. When he took that trip down the west coast of the South Island in 1846, he had lost all his money in the Nelson settlement and was being paid to be an explorer. Heaphy fulfilled many roles in the colonial spectrum: painter and sketcher (1839–1855); Commissioner of the Goldfields (Coromandel 1852–1853); Lieutenant in the Auckland Volunteer Rifles and Military Surveyor and Guide to the Forces on General Cameron's staff during the land wars of the 1860s; surveyor of the military road (later the Great South Road) for the invasion of the Waikato; first colonial winner of the Victoria Cross in an engagement near Te Awamutu in south-west Waikato in 1864 (an award regarded by Von Tempsky with jealous bitterness); Member of Parliament for Parnell (1867–1869); Commissioner of Native Reserves in the 1870s; Judge of the Native Land Court (1878–1880). His career is a roll call of colonial progress, of that progress which could turn its back to "tell the cities there was no such world." Though undoubtedly a better painter than Von Tempsky, he is not someone about whom a poem might be written called "Heaphy's Dance." His measured steps are those of the surveyor. His final escape was to Australia, where he died in Brisbane in 1881.

In Robin Hyde's imagining of Heaphy we get to see him "weighing his knowledge," perhaps as a prospector might weigh his gold. At the top of this final section of the poem, Hyde names two types of knowledge: "ghosts of dead men's knowledge" and "ghosts of young, rebellious, chidden knowledge" and describes knowledge itself as a "Dunce at its class" who is seen "stalking out of school." It is difficult to know if or how she connects these knowledges to Heaphy. Are the "ghosts of dead men's knowledge" meant to apply to the process of shaping and

42 Leggott, "Introduction," 1.

preparing the pounamu? What then does knowledge as a dunce refer to? The idea of knowledge itself being stupid, "tokanui," a Dunce, is a curious paradox, though attractive. That Hyde sums up the kind of knowledge Heaphy has discovered on his exploration as, "the thin precarious weight of early knowledge" might suggest it connects with knowledge as a young dunce. Heaphy stands confounded by what he sees. But then he turns away from it, "leaves" it as it were in Satchell's phrase, as if it had never been.

As if standing in such history, I've been trying here to raise the ghosts of "the thin precarious weight" of my own early knowledge and build it into a framework that can show how it changed and developed, from my growing up in Hamilton until the now in which I write; in other words, not turning away, but rather gazing backwards on that knowledge as it was when it was alive, as a "ghost of knowledge"—something each of us carries inside ourselves.

6 EPILOGUE: THE ESCAPE

Samuel Butler's colonial satire *Erewhon*, utilising his experience living in New Zealand from 1859 to 1864, was published in 1872 (Butler was back in England), just as the Belle Epoque began in the wake of the destruction of the Paris Commune; Satchell's *The Greenstone Door* was published in the unfortunate year of 1914 ("it was not the moment to have a compromised Pākehā-Māori character speak out against orthodox patriotism"[43]), as the Belle Epoque came to its catastrophic close. 1872 was the last year of sustained, if sporadic, armed conflict between Māori and Pākehā, that had continued for almost 30 years, since the early 1840s. In many ways the modern world was created during those years between 1872 and 1914—electricity, telephones, electrons and atomic structure, internal combustion, wireless, genetics, germ theory, film, flight and sound recording, just about everything we still rely on. The colonial trope of *Erewhon* is to create a "country within a country," a nowhere ("Erewhon") place you could stumble upon by following your wild thoughts over the hill. In the same way, for 20 years the Waikato contained a "country within a country" (Te Rohe Pōtae). The narrator of Butler's book stumbles into the imaginary place of Erewhon, but he ends up having to escape it, which he manages to do, along with his Erewhonian beloved Arowhena, in a balloon.

The narrator (whose name, we learn in the sequel *Erewhon Revisited*, is Higgs) and Arowhena (could her name mean something like "carefully thinking the thing through" in Māori? Butler's linguistic joke?) drift far out to sea and ditch in the

---

43 Kendrick Smithyman, "Satchell, William Arthur," accessed September 14, 2016, http://www.teara.govt.nz/en/biographies/3s4/satchell-william-arthur.

Pacific, where they are miraculously rescued by an Italian ship bound from Callao to Genoa. Higgs and Arowhena soon transfer to an English vessel sailing from Melbourne to London, and thus make their way "home." At the end of the book the narrator unveils his purpose in telling his story: he plans to return to Erewhon under the guise of a Christianising missionary purpose and either persuade (false inducements of fortunes to be made) or compel (a gunboat) the Erewhonians to be transported, in large numbers, as immigrant labourers to the sugar cane fields of Queensland. Thus will he make his fortune, selling human bodies and labour for profit, a Pacific "blackbirder," as they were known. Back in London, he notices an article in *The Times* that tells him Polynesians are already serving as forced labour in Queensland. It is 1872, Germany has just been united, the Communards have been slaughtered, Japan has responded to gunboat pressure by recently opening its doors, China is granting further "concessions" in the wake of the Opium Wars—*la Belle Epoque* is under way. In *The Times* the Marquis of Normanby, with regard to blackbird Polynesian labour, reassures that, "if one can judge by the countenances and manners of the Polynesians, they experience no regret at their position." After all, *The Times* concludes, those who have illegitimately acquired those Polynesians (as forced labourers) are going to "teach them religion" and that will "set at rest an[y] uneasy feeling."[44] Butler's satire rounds out by posing as an advertisement for a share float for his blackbirding colonial enterprise: "Please subscribe quickly. Address to the Mansion House, care of the Lord Mayor, whom I will instruct to receive names and subscriptions for me until I can organise a committee."[45] These are the last words of the novel.

Higgs escapes. Purcell, in *The Greenstone Door* does not; he is executed by the British military in a kangaroo court on fabricated charges of supplying arms to the Māori "rebels" slaughtered at Orakau. But Higgs' escape by balloon may not have been as effective as he hoped. Elsewhere in the book, Butler writes: "though this world looms so large when we are in it, it may seem a little thing when we have got away from it."[46] Higgs finds the world is smaller than he anticipated. His colonial enterprise may already have been trumped by the Pacific people themselves. He had initially set out on his adventure over the mountains with the help of a Māori guide going under the name of Chowbok (a nickname) or Kahabuka (Kahapuka?), who had fled the venture, in terror, at the point at which Higgs was about to enter the domain of Erewhon. Once Higgs has entered Erewhon and encountered the Erewhonians, he begins to speculate upon their origins and hits upon the notion "that they might be the lost ten tribes of Israel, of whom I had heard both my grandfather and my father make mention as existing in an unknown country, and awaiting a final return to

44   Samuel Butler, *Erewhon, or, Over the Range* (London: Jonathan Cape, 1932), 254.
45   Butler, *Erewhon*, 256.
46   Butler, *Erewhon*, 134.

Palestine."[47] Higgs persists in clinging tenaciously to this notion. He plans to reveal his discovery of the lost Israelites to the world in London. However in London he discovers none other than his old guide Chowbok, who is now presenting himself at a meeting at Exeter Hall on The Strand, rechristened after one of the minor prophets of the Old Testament as "the Rev. William Habakkuk," a "native missionary," about whom it is claimed "that the races of whom Mr Habakkuk was a specimen, were in all probability the lost ten tribes of Israel."[48]

At this point Butler's satire seems to return us to the wild shores of the Tattooed Rocks, and the speculation about Tamil or Arabic or Indian connections with Aotearoa. Is this native missionary cleverly selling a deal to gullible colonists in their own home country? Has Higgs' escape from Erewhon simply led him in a global circle back to the point of entering Erewhon, and is the book's final joke that there is no escape from the colonial condition, no way he can leave the "nowhere" place once it has been entered? But the connection with the lost tribes of Israel is possibly not as cranky as those extrapolations about the Tattooed Rocks. The earliest Māori prophet, the Nga Puhi tohunga Papahurihia (also known as Te Atua Wera) in the 1830s in his "early teachings in the Bay of Islands and Hokianga identified the Māori as Hurai, or Jews."[49] Papahurihia was the subject of a book length poem by Kendrick Smithyman, *Atua Wera*. Judith Binney points to the enduring significance of this identification with the Children of Israel: "Papahurihia's identification of the Māori with the Jews, and his use of the biblical serpent, Nakahi, . . . became important beliefs among Māori people."[50] Later prophets such as Te Kooti built on this identification which Binney notes bestows the power and the separateness of being "not Christians, but . . . the chosen of God."[51] This response to colonial intrusion creates something like "a religion inside a religion" somewhat similar to the idea of "a country within a country." The identification has never ceased and could be found in the later twentieth century in new manifestations such as the wholesale adoption of Rastafarianism by sections of Māori society and especially Māori music following Bob Marley and the Wailers single New Zealand concert on 16 April 1979. That Bob Marley's birthday was Waitangi Day must have seemed more than coincidence. In the second half of the 1980s Rastafarians near Ruatoria, going by the name of Ngati Dread, carried out a series of burnings of buildings, houses, farms and barns as acts of political resistance until their leader Chris Campbell was shot by a local farmer. Throughout this long imagining of

---

47 Butler, *Erewhon, or, Over the Range*, 57.
48 Butler, *Erewhon, or, Over the Range*, 255
49 Judith Binney, "Papahurihia, Penetana," accessed September 14, 2016, http://www.teara. govt.nz/en/biographies/1p4/papahurihia-penetana.
50 Binney, "Papahurihia."
51 Binney, "Papahurihia."

themselves as the Children of Israel in search of the Promised Land there has been a shared envisioning of a Canaan, a place that is not yet a place, a place yet to be reached and yet to be settled: a place to escape to.

In *The Dictionary of Imaginary Places* Alberto Manguel and Giasnni Guadalupi observe: "The world we call real has deadlocked boundaries in which the long-established principle that two bodies (let alone two mountains) cannot occupy the same place at the same time is rigorously observed. Our dictionary, however, deals with a more generous geography in which there is always room for one more town, island or kingdom."[52] The colonial endeavour starts out imagining a place without thinking that this will come to exist inside someone else's existing space. It is as if the real place that was imagined must become finally an imagined place in which "a more generous geography" obtains a real existence.

---

52 Alberto Manguel and Gianni Guadalupi, *The Dictionary of Imaginary Places* (San Diego: Harvest, 1999), xiii–xiv.

BIBLIOGRAPHY

Anderson, Atholl. "Retrievable Time: prehistoric colonisation of South Polynesia from the outside in and the inside out." In *Disputed Histories: Imagining New Zealand's Pasts*, edited by Tony Ballantyne and Brian Moloughney. Dunedin: Otago University Press, 2006.

Binney, Judith. "Papahurihia, Penetana." Accessed September 14, 2016. http://www.teara.govt.nz/en/biographies/1p4/papahurihia-penetana.

Butler, Samuel. *Erewhon, or, Over the Range*. London: Jonathan Cape, 1932 [1872].

Devlin, Pat. "Junats: young boots in the bush." *NZ Science Teacher* 108 (2005): 9–10.

Edmond, Murray. "Von Tempsky's Dance." Poem in *The Penguin Book of New Zealand Verse,* edited by Ian Wedde and Harvey McQueen, 504–505. Auckland: Penguin, 1985.

Hamilton, Scott. "Seven Urban Legends (for Murray Edmond)." *Brief* 47 (March 2013): 95–98.

Heaphy, Charles. "Notes of an Expedition to Kawatiri and Araura on the Western Coast of the Middle Island." In *Early Travellers in New Zealand*, edited by Nancy M. Taylor, 203–249. Oxford: Clarendon Press, 1959.

Hērangi, Te Puea. "E Noho, E Rata." Poem in *The Penguin Book of New Zealand Verse*, translated by Margaret Orbell and edited by Ian Wedde and Harvey McQueen, 133–134. Auckland: Penguin, 1985.

Howe, Kerry. "Māori/Polynesian Origins and the 'New Learning'." *Journal of the Polynesian Society* 108 (1999): 305–325.

--. *The Quest for Origins: Who First Discovered and Settled New Zealand and the Pacific Islands*. Auckland: Penguin, 2003.

Hunt, C.G. *Some Notes on the Mystery Wreck on Ruapuke Beach*. Hamilton: Waikato Scientific Association, 1955. Original held in Manuscript Collection MSC 15 Grayland, Hamilton Public Library.

Hyde, Robin. "Young Knowledge." Poem in *Young Knowledge: The Poems of Robin Hyde*, edited by Michele Leggott, 203–207. Auckland: Auckland University Press, 2003.

Laing, R.M., and E.W. Blackwell. *The Plants of New Zealand*, sixth ed. Christchurch: Whitcombe and Tombs, 1957.

Leggott, Michele. "Introduction." In *Young Knowledge: The Poems of Robin Hyde,* edited by Michele Leggott, 1–34. Auckland: Auckland University Press, 2003.

Manguel, Alberto, and Gianni Guadalupi. *The Dictionary of Imaginary Places*. Rev.ed. San Diego: Harvest, 1999 [Macmillan, 1980].

McMillan, N.A.C. "Story: Tempsky, Gustavus Ferdinand von." Accessed September 14, 2016. http://www.teara.govt.nz/en/biographies/1t90/tempsky-gustavus-ferdinand-von.

Nietzsche, Friedrich. *The Dawn of Day*, trans. J. M. Kennedy. London: T.N. Foulis, 1911.

--. *On Truth and Untruth: Selected Writings*, trans. Taylor Carman. Harper: New York, 2010.

--. *The Gay Science*, trans. Josefine Nauckhoff. Cambridge: Cambridge University Press, 2001.

--. *Writings from the Late Notebooks*, trans. Kate Sturge and ed. Rüdiger Bittner. Cambridge, UK: Cambridge UP, 2003.

O'Brien, Richard. *The Rocky Horror Show*. London: Samuel French, 1983.

Phillipps, W.J. "Incised Rocks, Raglan." *Journal of the Polynesian Society* 71, no. 4 (Dec. 1962): 400–402.

"Plastic Jesus." Authorship is most likely Ernie Marrs, Ed Cromarty and George Rush, who were the Goldcoast Singers. It seems likely that Marrs was the one who developed the song from two initial verses to its present size and shape. Accessed September 14, 2016. http://www.guntheranderson.com/v/data/plastic0.htm.

Satchell, William. *The Greenstone Door*. Auckland: Golden Press, 1980 [1914].

Smithyman, Kendrick. "Satchell, William Arthur." Accessed September 14, 2016. http://www.teara.govt.nz/en/biographies/3s4/satchell-william-arthur.

--. "Waikato Railstop." Poem in *Selected Poems,* edited by Peter Simpson, 55. Auckland: Auckland University Press, 1989.

Wells, Rufus. "An Unnatural History." *Landfall* 180 (Dec. 1991).

Wikipedia. "Gustvaus von Tempsky." Accessed September 14, 2016. https://en.wikipedia.org/wiki/Gustavus_von_Tempsky.

FROM *MEMORY CARDS: ALBERT SAIJO SERIES*

SUSAN M. SCHULTZ

LANGUAGE IS A BODY OF SUFFERING we carry on our backs like a woman a bloody girl. He was meant to fight in that war, but he declined. Decades later—it felt like going back, all those scenes in his head—he climbed a mountain in Vietnam. On that mountain he encountered an old woman who'd come to him in dreams, bearing a child through his sleep. Someone writes to me about the word "residue," how it lives in the DMZ between what is remembered and forgotten. He is arguing with a woman he loves but shares no language with. Ed Bradley still stands on Hamburger Hill. I can't recall his words, only his lips moving to the sound of gunfire. The old woman told him why he was there. That was knowledge he doesn't pass on.

—17 February 2011

I HURT THEREFORE I AM a memory-bearing substance, caught out on a limb like a temporal vagrant in a park full of banyans and bins. Analogy is not anodyne, nor is its nemesis. In pain, I remembered bathtubs, mirrors, furniture, lost persons, a stuffed bear. Each thing was like itself, if ghosted. He likes him some limitations, counting syllables to exert pressure on what is not his. Pull back behind the barricades, it's 1848, but in a different place. Or, it's 1932 and I've got pencils to sell. The lotus-eaters call to us but we've got to escape the time-warped casino. My metaphors vines that trip me as I walk the steep decline. Put down the memory mask, the satyr's horns, the snakes, the swords. This is for real.

—18 February 2011

BEAUTIFUL BIG SKY COUNTRY HIGH PLATEAU SURROUNDED BY MTS. The girl in pink roller skates found a railroad track leading inland from the Expo Center toward Minidoka. She worries about ducks who live in the water against which we're warned. Silhouetted bellies, an arc of geese under cloud, marshland reclaimed from mortal flood. The sign tells us workers got health care. It sits beside a dog park; a deaf woman tells us police are claiming the park for a training center. She's going to write a letter. *Positively no trespassing,* reads another sign. When someone's certain she remembers, the psych professor says, she's wrong. When I talk to the deaf woman, she responds. I cannot talk to Henry Kaiser on his sign; history renders him deaf, me dumb. He looks out at the grass, the dog walkers, the few tourists. He cannot hear the truck route, or the trains.

For Jessica Wahnetah
—25 February 2011

IF FORM IS EMPTY AND EMPTY FORM, then this thermos—before the coffee's poured—is the form of heat without its content. Coffee is content without carafe, spilling over on a book or homework page, an arbitrary stain. Sign on the straight line with whatever name is easiest to recall. Recall the governor. Recall the present to retrofit the past for what you know is coming, is. The bridges of Portland each have named structures: arches, beams, draw—, if not suspensions. Suspension is what we fear, the way it sets up shop in doubt, offers us a blizzard that's gone in an hour, moves without getting there. There's always a there in airplane travel, but liminal spaces take time. What I remember of that flight were its circles, and the labyrinth they walked, she in pink pants, he in matching shoes, looking for boundaries as much as the center we anyways saw. Time takes them away; I take my time. The former is more true than the latter. I am taken by it, but what I improvise will be my riff and bridge.

—5 March 2011

OUR SPIRIT EVER BUOYANT AS WE SINK, where sinking marks an upward curve, like unemployment or the debt ceiling. An economy of envy pays in emotion only, and they are not good wages. The public sector full of avarice, millionaires suffer at the hands of the tax man who keeps threatening to come. He's on his way, but the cell phone's dead and his GPS points to Kalihi, not Kahala. You can't climb the Koʻolau; they're too brittle, ridges too narrow to stand on. Gravity is a magnet, Bryant explains, that holds us to this globe no matter where we are. But we rise against it, flying like a boy clutching his balloons, an old man seated in his house float. The house is mortgaged against the land it leaves behind. It's the fault line, the default line, we barricade ourselves against. Do not covet our weightlessness; it is ours only. The guards have their orders.

—6 March 2011

WAKE UP WITHOUT A SENSE OF AGE: she's doing well, always nods and says "thank you"; they take her to the community center more these days. *Due to the events of the past weekend at _____, many individuals have expressed confusion and concern.* "War is uncertain—a thing where surprises are routine," reads Rumsfeld's snowflake. *We might need minefields on demand,* says another. In my dream, I congratulated him for becoming a father; he said he didn't want a child. But the dream has no sense of age either, is the cloud into which all our information flows. *Address these issues before they take on a life of their own.* He tells me about a prisoner, 72 years old, stuffed inside a suicide shirt, who screams in Khmer that someone is beheading him. His mother, and mine, wake up with their heads intact; who knows where to locate their mind-fields. The missing limbs line up at Angkor Wat to ask for change. His work ID reads EMBRACE CHANGE. She and she can't make it any more.

For Steve Weiss
—7 March 2011

AGING IS EVEN WORSE THAN DEATH but then how would we know, since the frame of our aging is at least made of wood? When I said "focal point," I gestured to my forehead; my colleague puts a hand to his ear when he speaks. That's the language center of the brain, the professor says. My mother leans to her right, elbow failing to catch the chair's arm. She falls outside the frame we call "sitting," like a student trying to conceal her texts. A cable channel "leans forward." My cabbie in Portland listens to his GPS speak Russian, but we still got lost, even as we keep driving ahead. The frame is a direction, though it turns back on itself. Death is what lives outside the frame. Our focus is automatic, especially as it blurs.

—8 March 2011

I AM BARKING TO BE LET OUT—rain a translucent grid, water retaining light against the greens. Our forests are not a solid green. Radhika's never still; in her absence I see soccer ball, hula skirt, stack of pastels, construction paper. My labyrinth waves like anemone in the denser air of March. He took the month, troped it into politics, denounced the natives for their protest. I knew when he used the word "landscape" her vote was lost. He said culture cannot exist beyond the page, that the page is what matters. Work the words, like a field tilled until it yields a crop to itself alone. My mother loses her culture, and that's how I know she had one. In anger, she'd fall quiet. Her bark a joyful noise. I would stash it in a box, save it for a rainy day, take it for a walk, pick up its shit, pat its furry head, let it sleep by the television. Leave the truth commissions to us.

—9 March 2011

I AM A REED THAT CEPHALIZED & GREW LIMBS. I am out on one. I dangle, therefore I am. SHE calls to ask if anyone with health insurance is willing to marry an HIV-positive man without. SHE tells me SHE'S drinking too much. SHE tells me HE hates his job, but HE says nothing to ME in words. SHE wonders why HER name was changed once, then not again. HE worries HIS birth-father is not long for this world. I need a bath after the meeting, HIS machine-gun ressentiment. HE writes about "the whole child," but WE'RE in a Poe story and OUR tower contains an eye (a real one). OUR house is inhabited by a ghost stronger than ourselves. THE WOMEN will eat you and THE MEN write beautiful sentences.

—10 March 2011

AUTHOR'S NOTE

Each of these memory cards begins from a sentence or a phrase from Albert Saijo's *OUTSPEAKS: A RHAPSODY*, published by Bamboo Ridge Press in 1997.

THE HISTORY OF THE HAY(NA)KU

EILEEN TABIOS

[Less than two years after I publicly inaugurated the hay(na)ku, *The First Hay(na)ku Anthology* was co-published in 2005 by Meritage Press (St. Helena & San Francisco, U.S.A.) and xPress(ed) (Espoo, Finland). Reflecting the hay(na)ku's continued popularity, *The Hay(na)ku Anthology, Vol. 2* (2008) was released just three years after the first anthology. These first two anthologies were co-edited by Mark Young and Jean Vengua. Two years after the second anthology, *THE CHAINED HAY(NA)KU PROJECT* anthology was released in 2010, curated by Ivy Alvarez, John Bloomberg-Rissman, Ernesto Priego and Eileen Tabios. This third anthology differs from the earlier ones by focusing on collaborations involving at least three poets and/or artists.

In addition to the three anthologies, the hay(na)ku also has appeared in other anthologies, numerous journals and many single-author poetry collections. I fully expect the hay(na)ku's popularity to continue to grow. Its progress can be tracked through the online links of http://eileenrtabios.com/haynaku/ and http://haynakupoetry.blogspot.com. The following is an essay about its history, first printed in the now out-of-print *The First Hay(na)ku Anthology*.]

In September 2000, I began a "Counting Journal" with the idea that counting would "be just another mechanism for me to understand my days." That journal lasted for only five months because I could maintain its underlying obsession, which was to count everything, for only that long. It was inspired, as this first entry explained on September 20, by:

> Ianthe Brautigan's *You Can't Catch Death—A Daughter's Memoir* which noted the character Cameron in her father Richard Brautigan's *The Hawkline Monster*: "Cameron was a counter. He vomited nineteen times to San Francisco. He liked to count everything."

A month later, I would write:

> I am in library intending to finish reading in one seating Richard Brautigan's *An Unfortunate Woman*. From P. 77:
> "I've always had at times a certain interest in counting. I don't know why this is. It seems to come without a preconceived plan and then my

counting goes away. Often without me ever having noticed its departure.

I think I counted the words on the early pages of this book because I wanted to have a feeling of continuity, that I was actually doing something, though I don't know exactly why counting words on a piece of paper served that purpose because I was actually doing something.

Anyway, I stopped counting words on page 22 on February 1, 1982, with a total of 1,885 words. I hope that is the correct sum. I can count, but I can't add which, in itself, is sort of interesting."

Fast forward to June 10, 2003 where I am writing in my first poetics blog, "WINEPOETICS" at http://winepoetics.blogspot.com. On the blog, I'd been excerpting from the Counting Journal. At this point, I decide to write one last counting-related blog entry, which became:

But rather than spend more days having you witness me gazing into that part of my navel where Brautigan's eyes are twinkling back, let me write just one last Counting post. This one will feature snippets based on which page the journal opens to when I drop it on the floor. The idea came to me when … I dropped the journal on the floor as I was polishing off my 2nd glass of the 2001 Dutch Henry Los Carneros Chardonnay.

Drop Journal: Page opens onto 12/18/00. Bush secured Electoral College majority—271 votes—to become the U.S.' 43rd President. It was announced that Hillary Clinton received an $8.0 mio. advance for a memoir for her years in the White House. W/ Simon and Schuster. So much $ for tsismis, whereas one can't even find $5,000 to publish a poetry book!

Ugh. Close Journal. Drop Journal Again. Page opens onto 1/28/01: On plane returning to San Francisco, read *Selected Letters of Jack Kerouac*. P. 46—Kerouac says, "I think American haikus should never have more than 3 words in a line—e.g.

Trees can't reach
for a glass
of water"

I am inaugurating the Filipino Haiku [PinoyPoets: Attention! I'll post if you send me some!]: 3 lines each having one, two, three words in order—e.g.

Trees
can't reach
for a glass

. . .

Enough poets responded to my blog-post so that I was able to announce just two days later:

PHILIPPINE INDEPENDENCE DAY ~~ PINOY HAIKU

It seems most apt to introduce the "Pinoy Haiku" on June 12, Philippine Independence Day. This was the day in 1898 that General Emilio Aguinaldo proclaimed Philippine independence from Spain.

But soon afterwards, the United States—having just tasted, and found sweet, its entry as a world power into the arena of global politics—chose not to recognize the Philippines's successfully fought battle for self-determination. The U.S. invaded the Philippines to turn it into a colony. It wasn't until 1946 that the U.S. formally ended its colonial regime on a day coinciding with the U.S. Independence Day of July 4. Consequently, the Philippines only began to commemorate June 12 in the early 1960s when President Diosdado Macapagal changed Philippine Independence Day from the 4th of July to June 12...

Filipino poets responded to my call for the "Pinoy Haiku" with enthusiasm. Perhaps in part because, as Michelle Bautista pointed out, the idea of one-two-three "works with the Filipino nursery rhyme: *isa, dalawa, tatlo, ang tatay mo'y kalbo* (pronounce phonetically to catch the rhythm)—which translates into English as "one two three, your dad is bald."

Here are some fresh examples of the Pinoy Haiku, beginning with one written by Barbara Jane Reyes for Philippine Independence Day:

land
of the
mo(u)rning, i toast.

Barbara deftly conflates the reference of "land of the morning" from the Philippine national anthem with the wine theme of this WINEPOETICS blog. Relatedly, Patrick Rosal offers:

NYC PINOY BLUES OR
THE AY NAKU HAIKU

God-
damn—same
shit/different dog

Meanwhile, Leny M. Strobel and Oscar Peñaranda's contributions reflect both the events over a century ago as well as the current times (the U.S. had just invaded Iraq)—befitting their shared status as scholars/teachers as well as poets:

Freedom
Is Cheap
When You're Bushed
—*Leny M. Strobel*

Power
Drippingly exudes
And always stains
—*Oscar Peñaranda*

Here's two riffed off by Oliver de la Paz while he was doing laundry:

Keats
writes darkly.
Birds trill unseen.

Watches
around wrists
make teeth marks.

In these works, what's evident to me is that the charge associated with the haiku remains in the Pinoy form with the type of paradox that one might find in the Filipino *bagoóng*—a pungent fish sauce enjoyed by Filipinos but, ahem, misunderstood by non-Filipinos. Thus, does Catalina Cariaga also offer:

onion
just eaten;
smell my breath

• • •

Most of the Pinoy "haiku" (scare quotes deliberate) came from writers who belonged to Flips, a listserve of either Filipino writers or anyone interested in Filipino Literature that was co-founded by poets Nick Carbo and Vince Gotera. While my compadres and comadres happily sent me what Vince called these "Stairstep Tercets," my project also ended up eliciting a discussion on the implications of *Naming*—and how I was approaching it by using the phrase "Pinoy Haiku." Vince asked:

Appropriating the "haiku" name has all sorts of prosodic and postcolonial problems (by which I mean the WWII "colonizing" of the Philippines by Japan, among other things). Am I being overly serious here? When you say Kerouac refers to "American haiku" not having more than three words per line, I think he might have been reacting to Allen Ginsberg's "American sentence" which has 17 syllables per line. I guess my concern about calling it a "Pinoy haiku" is that readers could say "Hey, Pinoys can't even get the haiku right!" They won't always have the Kerouac quote to guide them. Besides, why must we always be doing things in reaction to the term "American"? An interesting parallel poetic-form-naming might be Baraka's "low coup" form (the diametrical opposite of "high coup" / haiku). Maybe the Pinoy version could be the "hay (na)ku"?

"Hay naku" is a common Filipino expression covering a variety of contexts—like the word "Oh."

Another poet had suggested that I also rename the project because the traditional haiku form should be respected. Well, yes and no. As I told that poet—I also think that, in Poetry, rules are sometimes made to be broken.

And, I initially wasn't moved either by Vince's notion as regards Japan "colonizing" the Philippines during WWII. If anything, I thought that were I to move down that line of thinking (which I hadn't been), I didn't mind subverting the Japanese haiku form specifically because I thought of it as *talking back* against Japanese imperialism. But, on closer consideration, I realized that the perspective could work both ways ... and that using the "haiku" reference also could imply a continuation of "colonial mentality."

Catalina "Catie" Cariaga also appreciated Vince's comments:

> Hey Vince, I like "hay(na)ku." That's the spirit! Like halo-halo. There's a chapter in Vicente Rafael's *Contracting Colonializm* about that guy Pin Pin who translated the Spanish grammar book into the Filipino vernacular—which ended taking all types of forms, songs, explanations and translations—perhaps to SUBVERT the very project he was assigned to "translate." I read Rafael's comments very seriously. Pin Pin used combinations of long languid fluid lines and short syllabic bursts. We have those kinds of macro and micro-rhythms in our F(P)ilipino American repertoire. Like halo-halo.

Vicente's observations, indeed, should be read by many. But, with all due respect to Vicente, I also found Catie's reply most persuasive due to the reference to halo-halo:

an incredibly yummy-licious Filipino dessert of shaved ice, coconut shavings, bits of fruit jello and tropical fruits like jackfruit, banana ... I'ma getting hungry ...

Anyway, I bowed to Vince's wisdom (he is, after all, older than I am; wink here at Vince) and renamed the form "HAY(NA)KU."

. . .

Since the birth of hay(na)ku, there has been a hay(na)ku contest judged by Barbara Jane Reyes which was quite popular in the internet's poetry blogland; the hay(na)ku form was taught by Junichi P. Semitsu, then Director of "June Jordan's Poetry for the People" program at the African American Studies Department at U.C. Berkeley; and many other poets—non-Filipino as well as Filipino—have picked up the form to write it as I originally conceived as well as to offer variations.

Maya Mason Fink, the 11-year-old daughter of poet Thomas Fink, concocted a variation whereby the first line has one word of one letter, the second line two words of two letters each, the third line three words of three letters each, and so on—as far as the poet wishes to take it. "The Mayan Hay(na)ku" points to one of the hay(na)ku's possibilities as an attractive tool for introducing poems to youngsters.

Kari Kokko introduced a "moving hay(na)ku" via the internet whereby, through the wonders of HTML, the lines move across the screen. Thomas Fink, a painter as well as a poet, also completed a painting series that presents his visual manifestation of the hay(na)ku. Other hay(na)ku variations include the "Ducktail Hay(na)ku" whose ducktail references a hairstyle that shows a thin strand of hair trailing down from an otherwise shortly-cropped hair cut; this version features the three-line stanza, followed by another one-line stanza of any length. Another variation is the "Reverse Hay(na)ku" whereby the numbering of words per line is 3, 2 and 1, respectively, versus 1, 2 and 3. One of the most effective variations has been the hay(na)ku sequence, as epitomized in the works of Kirsten Kaschock, Sheila Murphy, harry k stammer, Tom Beckett, Ernesto Priego and many other poets. Some of these sequences are included in this anthology. Others, as the hay(na)ku continues to develop and spread as a poetic form, have been written since submissions and considerations closed, and have appeared elsewhere.

At the time of writing this essay, Scott Glassman is introducing the "abecedarian hay(na)ku" sequence whereby each word begins with each succeeding letter of the English alphabet.

As one can see by the history of the hay(na)ku, it is a community-based poetic form which fits my own thoughts on the poem as a space for engagement. "Community" is a word laden with much baggage—both good and bad. I, too, have a conflicted reaction to the word. But I have to say that some of my favorite poetic projects are those where I consciously am building towards a community—through both poetic form and content. Why? Because I think a poem doesn't fully mature without a particular community called reader(s). Poetry is (inherently) social.

. . .

Since the initial response by Filipino poets to the hay(na)ku, many—if not most—hay(na)ku have been written by non-Filipinos. This is certainly a fine result since Poetry is not (or need not be) ethnic-specific. But I'm also glad that non-Filipinos have taken up this form because I consider the hay(na)ku to be both a Filipino as well as Diasporic Poetic.

In the diaspora, the Filipino meets many influences and what would be the point of denying such? Given that the diaspora has existed throughout Filipino history, to call something "Filipino," in my view, is not the same as hearkening back only to so-called "indigenous" Filipino traits. I agree with Filipino poet Eric Gamalinda when he observes, "The history of the Philippines is the history of the world."

. . .

Ironically, I actually feel myself mostly mediocre at the hay(na)ku. I've written just a few as of the time of preparing this anthology, such as this while potty-training my puppy Achilles:

HERE WE GO AGAIN
"by" Achilles

"Go
Potty!" Mama
exhorts. Sigh. Poop.

But I also think it's appropriate that I, presumably the hay(na)ku's "inventor," may be mediocre at this form. I think this logical because I've long felt that Poetry ultimately transcends the poet's autobiography. Even when the narrative offers up elements of my own life, I consider the poem a space of engagement with others, with the results being nothing I can either predict or control. In this sense, the hay(na)ku very much retains my person-hood, even as its outcomes are based on others.

For the hay(na)ku, as with any of my poems, all I can do is offer my hand and hope that someone ultimately will grasp it. For the hay(na)ku, I feel as if the entire universe wreathed itself about that writing hand. Thank you, All.

July 31, 2005
St. Helena, California

FROM *FROM UNINCORPORATED TERRITORY [GUMA']*

CRAIG SANTOS PEREZ

FROM FATAL IMPACT STATEMENTS [READER'S GUIDE]

GLOSSARY:

CONTROLLED ACCESS : area where public access is prohibited or limited due to periodic training operations—

DEPRESSION : low-pressure tropical weather system with rotary circulation and rain—

ACTIVITY : individual scheduled training action such as missile launching bombardment vehicle driving or field carrier landing practice—

TROPICAL STORM : tropical cyclone with distinct circulation and wind speeds of 39 to 73 miles per hour—

AIRSPACE, CONTROLLED :

TYPHOON : tropical cyclone with strong pronounced rotary winds and sustained surface winds of 74 miles per hour—

AIRSPACE, UNCONTROLLED :

SUPERTYPHOON : tropical cyclone with sustained wind speed over 149 miles per hour—

AIRSPACE : space lying above land or water such as the pacific ocean—more specifically the space lying above a nation and coming under its jurisdiction—

READINESS : ability of forces, units, and weapon systems to perform—includes
   ability to deploy and employ without delays—

ORGANIZE : [www.weareguahan.com]—

CONDITION OF READINESS 4 : damaging winds may arrive on island within 72
   hours—

MANEUVER : movement of forces in combination with fire—

DEBRIS : secure all loose items that could become airborne during high winds—

RANGE : area designated and equipped for firing lines and positions, maneuver
   areas, firing lanes, test pads, detonation pads, impact areas—

CONDITION OF READINESS 3 : damaging winds may arrive within 48 hours—
   prepare household for long-term power and water loss—

FORCE FLOW : rate at which military personnel dependents and civilian workers
   will arrive—

NO-ACTION ALTERNATIVE :

POINT OF CONTACT :   Joint Guam Program Office
                     c/o Naval Facilities Engineering Command, Pacific
                     Attn: Guam Program Management Office
                     258 Makalapa Drive, Suite 100
                     Pearl Harbor, HI 96860

BASE LOAD POWER : minimum generation capacity needed to meet continuous demand for the system—

INTERIOR : stay inside even when eye of typhoon is passing and all appears to be calm—

CONDITION OF READINESS 2 : damaging winds may arrive within 24 hours— seek emergency shelter if home is not prepared to withstand damaging winds—

U.S. TERRITORIAL WATERS : sea areas within twelve nautical miles of coastline—

CUMULATIVE IMPACT : impact of action when added to past present and future actions—

DISTANCE X : maximum distance projectile will travel when fired at given elevation with given charge—

MITIGATION :

FREEDOM OF ACTION :

CONDITION OF READINESS 1 : damaging winds are occurring or expected within 12 hours—

IMPACT AREA : area intended to capture munitions or explosives and debris fragments—

FROM FATAL IMPACT STATEMENTS [EXECUTIVE SUMMARY]

forced
flow

[final environmental impact statement 2010]
[draft environmental impact statement 2009]

'us will maintain forward deployed forces to deter situations for defense of japan

[agreement between government of us and government of japan concerning implementation of relocation of iii marine expeditionary force personnel and dependents from okinawa to guam—
guam international agreement 2009]

'us operations must respond when an armed attack has occurred against defenses of japan
[us-japan roadmap for realignment implementation—'roadmap' 2006]

'us strike capabilities and nuclear deterrence remain essential to ensuring defense of japan
[us-japan alliance transformation and realignment agreement 2005]

'us will provide all necessary support for defense of japan
[us-japan treaty of mutual cooperation and security—mutual security treaty 1960]

construction tempo and
sequencing

• • •

dispersal threats *[us navy to fund increase of federally funded brown tree snake interdiction measures related to direct indirect and induced growth caused by marine corps relocation to guam]*

dispersal threats *[since 1983 eight brown tree snake sightings on oahu hawaiʻi— last sighting in 1998 brown tree snake found dead within wheel well of continental airlines flight]*

• • •

'moving forces to guam would place them on westernmost   furthest forward

       sovereign
us territory in the pacific capable of
supporting such a
presence

thereby maximizing 'freedom
of action'
while minimizing
increased response time relative
to previous stationing
in okinawa'

dispersal threats *[snake dispersal pathways associated with buildup include travel on commercial aircraft cargo on aircraft cargo on military and commercial seagoing vessels]*

dispersal threats *[us navy will not fund increased interdiction measures identified more than one year after end of marine corps relocation construction and conclusion of relocation to guam]*

FROM FATAL IMPACT STATEMENTS
[VOLUME TWO : MARINE CORPS RELOCATION]

A sound is perceived as gunfire. Waves cause sound to crash against the shore. Sound is the stimulation of auditory organs produced by waves transmitted through the air or through words. Natural and unmade sources. Sound waves are pressure fluctuations caused by voices. Sound waves move outward from the vibration source and echo through the interior. When military planes fly overhead, we can't hear each other. We wait for them to pass; cover our ears. Echoes also occur due to wind, ground cover, and migration. Sound waves pressure bodily organs. Loudness measures the loss of sound. A sound can't be unmade if it's natural, it can only be silenced. I want the sound of our voices to rise. Noise is unwanted sound sometimes based on trauma. Noise comes from natural and manmade sources. Live fire training. Noise causes adverse effects on physical and psychological health. Military personnel make noise in bars, strip clubs, and massage parlors. Some military weapons can kill you before you hear them. The degree to which a sound is perceived to be noise depends on context. Our voices are oceanic waves. You can hear sound when standing at its source, but eventually you will disappear. Words are pulsing sound waves and bodily organs. Through words, we can move the air.

FROM FATAL IMPACT STATEMENTS
[VOLUME TWO : MARINE CORPS RELOCATION]

from exstirpare "root out" *from* ex- "out" and stirps "a root trunk of a tree"
extirpation [n] extirpative [adj] extirpator [n]

extirpate [v] : to pull
up by the roots   ~~mariana fruit bat | fanihi~~

to undo
as if from the roots   ~~mariana crow | aga~~

to destroy completely as if
down to the roots   ~~guam micronesian kingfisher | sihek~~

to cause to move
into a new   ~~guam rail | koko~~

position or place—
'removal'—   ~~micronesian starling | sali~~

      'recovery habitats on lands proposed for use under proposed action'

to uproot
to surgically remove   ~~mariana swiftlet | chuchaguak~~

an organ or part
as if within the roots   ~~mariana common moorhen | palattat~~

to remove something concrete
through the roots   ~~mariana eight spot butterfly | ababang~~

to remove something abstract
no longer present

in the wild
'have been extirpated from guam'   *repeat*

FROM FATAL IMPACT STATEMENTS
[VOLUME TWO : MARINE CORPS RELOCATION]

a militarized ars poetica

visual resources include
scenic areas vistas or locations that
provide natural appearing or
aesthetically pleasing views
such as shorelines seascapes cliffs
and man-made views unique buildings

landscaping and national parks
typically visual resource descriptions
focus on *highly valued* tourist views
however visual resources are also
views people are accustomed to
seeing and often take for granted

visual resources are important to
sensory experience of an area
users encounter space foremost
through visual interaction with a 'view'
[foreground middle-ground and
background] for analysis

visual resources are composed of
dominant landscape features
diversity of line color form texture
distinctive visual edges
visual quality judged by its vividness
[memorability of landscape components

striking or distinctive patterns]
its intactness [integrity of visual order
in view and freedom from visual
encroachment] and unity [visual coherence
of harmonious patterns] the proposed
action will substantially alter

quality of significant vistas view-sheds
or overlooks will change the light
glare and shadows within a given area
and substantially affect viewers
as in all things aesthetic
there's a subjective component

PACIFIC RIM: INDIFFERENT PASTORALISM

COREY WAKELING

At a poetics reading group meeting in 2011, Ann Vickery, Australian poet and critic, author of *Stressing the Modern: Cultural Politics in Australian Women's Poetry* (2007) and poetry collection *Devious Intimacy* (2015), shared a portion of Jed Rasula's *This Compost: Ecological Imperatives in American Poetry* (2002) for study in the context of Australian ecopoetics. They were familiar with *This Compost*, but I had only heard of it at the time. But reading Rasula's materialist engagement with poetics on paper as composts within contradictory histories and geographies excited me in its treatment of literary culture as wilderness. However, in doing so, Rasula does not simply jettison the idea of mind. Mind instead becomes networked with other ecological processes, with poetic consciousness developed on paper being as relevant to eco-thinking as other consciousness developed in other practical activities, such as botany or hiking. Rasula's *This Compost* tacitly endorsed what in poetry I had thought I was adventuring: a materially fluid conception of writing that pulsed between life and record, and back again. Inscription, in this general view, is no less textual, and amounts less to a diminution of its literary and conceptual powers than a revivification of a transhistorical view of writing as a living material force. In an earlier book with Steve McCaffery, Rasula and McCaffery offer a theory which openly dismisses the kinds of theories which close off this porosity of language viewed in the world, entertaining the delightful idea of language as a negotiation of "membership in the world":

> Language forms and performs our membership in the world, melting a resistant reality into pliable accessibility while at the same time producing and inducing distance, deferral, difference; so that there is always a new discrepancy to overcome by yet another act of signification, and each sign tendered to fill the gap creates another gap.[1]

Insofar as ecology is incredulous to the whims of the private archive called the mind, Rasula braves an engagement with literary thinking, and literary history's thinking of the environment, as an ecologically networked repository of thought. In Rasula's words, the poem may thus be viewed as "a space possessed of a nature,

---

1 Jed Rasula and Steve McCaffery, eds., *Imagining Language: An Anthology* (Cambridge, Massachusetts and London, England: The MIT Press, 1998), 472.

which absorbs 'symbol detritus' like the photosynthesis of light in chlorophyll."[2] This tensile, physical, microbial view of writing resonates specifically with the ways in which I have archived the environmental specificities of locations defined by their difference across the Ring of Fire, also known as the Pacific. Namely, in my poetics, an abandoned love song to Eyjafjallajökull in the series *36 Views* which I have published from, but never in full, as well as a broader interest in environmentalism as a way of radical thinking, begin to make sense when querying questions of environment and poetry offered by Rasula. Complementary modes of writing theorized in the work of poet critic Joyelle McSweeney and amateur volcanologist Masao Mimatsu coordinate a notion of ecological writing wherein mind is deindividualized. What I discover in this convergence of ideas is an expressivity indifferent to the health of the subject, but concerned with the emergence of new flows with the Pacific Rim as its site. Geographical and geological differences arise out of a diversity of environmental signs stemming from tectonic and volcanic activity. My encounter in the middle of this convergence makes legible how geological difference in Australian and Japanese contexts might differently impact upon practice.

One area of inquiry in *This Compost* is the concept "ecology of the mind" coined by Gregory Bateson. Importantly, Bateson's human subject is a different agent of selfhood than presented by the Romantic poets Samuel Taylor Coleridge and William Wordsworth in their treatises, even as the latter two are understood to be more ecological than their Augustan forebears. Wordsworth, for example, writes that the human mind exists: "... as naturally the mirror of the fairest and most interesting qualities of nature."[3] Instead of a mimetic mind like Wordsworth's ideal poetic subject, one of concordance and agreeability through which nature appears in its essences, Bateson's ecology of mind as applied by Rasula leads us to Thomas Browne in the *Religio Medici* and "Nature, that universall and publik Manuscript" but also Walt Whitman's, "gusty-temper'd little whiffet, *man*, that runs indoors at a mite of rain or snow."[4] Bateson's conception of the mind as ecological thus imprecates those versions of the human subject that runs from rain or snow, or would seek to understand nature via distance. Mind as wagered by Rasula is, on the one hand, like some kind of unfolding universal manuscript, a book from which all others dis-locate, and on the other, seemingly if utterly dislocated from his book runs in fear back indoors by signs of those permutations of nature that would

---

2 Jed Rasula, *This Compost: Ecological Imperative in American Poetry* (Athens: University of Georgia Press, 2002), 197.

3 William Wordsworth, from the 'Preface to Lyrical Ballads, with Pastoral and Other Poems (1802),' in *The Norton Anthology of English Literature: The Romantic Period*, ed. Stephen Greenblatt (New York: W.W. Norton & Company, 2006), 271.

4 Walt Whitman, *Specimen Days & Collect* (New York: Dover Publications, 1995), 89–90. My italics.

penetrate tranquillity. Rasula is most interested in Bateson's concept of mind's implications for selfhood in relation to ecology, since for Rasula the "individual mind is immanent but not only in the body ... immanent also in pathways and messages outside the body ..."[5] That is, mind is discoverable in all things. Mind can be extrapolated from networks of expression. Mind can be found in processes that make networks of expression as well as be the result of individual agents within networks. Thus, the cosmology implicates, "a larger mind in which the individual mind is only a subsystem."[6] One can read such a cosmology as pre-modern, the province of pantheisms to whom the individual mind is but a substrate of a larger collective or omnipotent mind. However, to read it in such a way is to overlook the inclusion of "pathways and messages" as two-way faculties of the mind in its connexion to the world. "[P]athways and messages" too evokes the membrane, a kind of Latourian "compositionist" agent within a larger, more than human network.[7] Thus, to speak in the way Rasula endorses we do after Bateson is to see poetry writing as a material endeavour embedded in ecological circumstances. As Rasula quotes of "Whitman's Ontario devotee Dr. Bucke," viewed ecologically, mind can be understood as a "subsystem."[8]

If the individualised mind is a locus or node of pathways and messages, then the Romantic wanderer above sea and fog in a contemporary ecopoetical frame has been swallowed by that diaphanousness of the glowing alpine purview, and is coming to resemble it. Walt Whitman in the same 'specimen' of *Specimen Days* mentioned earlier writes that the trees "do as well as most speaking, writing, poetry, sermons—or rather they do a great deal better. Go and sit in a grove or woods, with one or more of those voiceless companions, and read the foregoing, and think."[9] Such a reading of phenomenology emphasizes a shifted consciousness of where mind is found. For Whitman here, consciousness is to be found in the wilderness. More specifically, what we have arrived at is not a mind thinking at all, but an ecology doing the thinking. The temporality of deep ecology demands we consider everything that predetermines us, an interdependence of excrement and blossom, CO_2 to O_2, appearance as the consequence of decay. Old ideas of mind in the context of poetry become obsolete when we take on the implications of writing as part of a larger organic, autopoietic palimpsest of times and things: compost. If every ecosystem relies on manifold interrelated processes of excrement and fertility, fertilisation and consumption, excretions of enzymes and indurations of flesh for surfaces, and

---

5 Rasula, *This Compost*, 3.
6 Ibid.
7 See Bruno Latour, "An Attempt at a 'Compositionist' Manifesto," *New Literary History* 41 (2010), 471–490.
8 Rasula, *This Compost*, 3.
9 Whitman, *Specimen Days & Collect*, 90.

pheromones, stigma, proteins and calcites for orifices and membranes, then every self, now a particular set of membranes and not at all a genius, is constituted by the cross-communication of self-fertilising entities. Composts. Soils. The human, we might then revise, is uniquely the compost for which compost is a concern. What we require for life, that which predicates us and begins the reflexes—for the child just born this is the lungs' encounter with air—though unconscious for "man the mirror" of Wordsworth, is indifferently essential.

That ecology has something to say *about* poetry's extended life, not just something to say *for* poetry, is to my mind an obvious thing which still might be said more clearly. This supplanting of the self in poetry with a consuming, fertilising node of a larger system, endows poetics an exigency toward sensitivity and vitality, and the sense that language is a bacterium. That we as poets be interactive and interdependent soils, also, for our own health, means in our formation we must account for all of our excreta and collateral of production. Moreover, for the self to be replaced with an ecology in poetics, poetry then becomes a gauge of inter-ecological and intellectual health. The inoperative, the diseased and the industrially poisoned compost is expressive, you know it from your own failures at home. Stagnant, compost grows mould; accidentally mix meat scraps in it and the rats come to feed. Interestingly, this concept includes the urban; as termites make castles of excrement so too do we live in towers constructed of matter masticated by external digesting apparatus. As we are constructed of our "pathways and messages" so too our minds appear as intelligent design in our networks, and more exactly, as collaborations with world and collectivity. Moreover, we in fact exist as lively topsoil, parasites of the decay and vitality of the past.

Poet Joyelle McSweeney, in a theory of "the necropastoral," inadvertently applies the poetics of compost but via a larger theory of poetry as a material phenomena flouting divides between life and death, with a necrotic view of idealism a central cause.[10] The environmentalism within this theory is a corporeal stage. McSweeney, writing about the poetry of Kim Hyesoon, for example, describes how "from within the landfill, on the loops and arcs of poison ... [appears] a special, doomed body."[11] Mind becomes a less critical concern for McSweeney in such theorisation than the body. What is implicitly transcendental materialism participates in a broader critique of Descartes, a critique which alchemist philosopher Thomas Browne raised in a clear denunciation of those who would seek their limited religious ideas in the

---

10   I quote from McSweeney's original online essays, but the larger theory has since been developed into a book: Joyelle McSweeney, *The Necropastoral: Poetry, Media, Occults* (Ann Arbor: University of Michigan Press, 2014).

11   Joyelle McSweeney, "Garbage In/Garbage In the Necropastoral: On the Road to Kimp'o Landfill: Kim Hyesoon & Camile Rose Garcia & Césaire," in *Montevidayo* (2011), accessed September 10, 2016, http://www.montevidayo.com/?p=1255#more-1255.

infinitude of nature and quoted in Rasula, imprecating those: "who cast a more carelesse eye on these common Hieroglyphicks [of nature], and disdain to suck Divinity from flowers ..."[12] In McSweeney's words, opposing the divide between the eye and the flowers: "the membrane separating the Pastoral from the Urban, the past from the future, the living from the dead, may and must be supersaturated, convulsed, and crossed. This membrane is Anachronism itself. Another name for it is Death, or Media."[13] Today's "carelesse eye[s]" come from the inflexible hermeneuts for whom fertility, or natural health, is a fixed category.

The necropastoral, by contrast, proffers a creative technology or discourse which razes the wicket between nectar and the wilting calyx, between the sunlit pasture and the dark woods, between the compost and the plant, and discovers in those interstices the relations of membranes. The idea of the membrane, though use it as you wish in the context of ecology, is applied in a Deleuzian manner (indebted to Gilbert Simondon): "The living lives at the limit of itself, on its limit. ... The characteristic polarity of life is at the level of the membrane; it is here that life exists in an essential manner."[14] A membrane is still a divide, but it is a living and erogenous one, through which things transform. If it does not open to life, it remains a cordon of the dead, or the unborn. Art, and poetry in particular, is herein induced to approach ecology by experimenting on it (supersaturation), reanimating it (convulsing), and trespassing on it or penetrating it (crossing). This kind of membrane is not just one mediated by contaminatory human practices, but experimented with by the Pacific Rim itself, tectonically and volcanically. The very terms of health and death, contamination and rejuvenation, are set by the environmental conditions spewed out in magma and pyroclast. McSweeney's theory helps remind us of *Et in Arcadia Ego*, that who but death also lives in the pastoral, a conceit commonly found in pastoral paintings by the likes of Francesco Guercino and Nicolas Poussin.

Between Rasula and McSweeney, the relation between poetry and ecology is positioned much the same. Both by implication view poetic thinking as escalated by a richer notion of ecological connectivity and the material flexibility of subjective apprehensions of objects, namely, that such relations exceed the subject and interpretation. If tonality and aesthetic preference do not fully explain the difference between the two adequately enough, it is because those terms are not ecologically binding; Gaia remains indifferent to questions of metonymy versus manifesto, or permaculturalist versus goth. Rather, their difference lies in the compositional role poetry plays in extending the ecological decentring of the subject. This difference flags an important paradox produced by compositional and decompositional emphases

---

12 Rasula, *This Compost*, 1.
13 Joyelle McSweeney, "Necropastoral, or, Normal Love," in *Montevidayo* (2011), accessed September 10, 2016, http://www.montevidayo.com/?p=788.
14 Gilles Deleuze, *The Logic of Sense*, trans. Mark Lester (London: Continuum, 2009), 119.

available to the basically inhuman, post-anthropocentric quality of compost. That is, there are good and bad ways to compost, yet the temporality by which we extrapolate what rate of decay and production is good for the ferment is actually as anthropocentric as any other agricultural, pastoral orientation towards compost. Adjudged by geological time, to the contrary, we start to surpass the scale of composts at hand for the human, to invoke Heidegger's term for the role prehensility has in subjectivity, and enter into a frame which glides forward on the cosmologies like Rasula's and McSweeney's, but inevitably necessitate the supersession of the sphere of human composition. This is the paradox: Rasula and McSweeney imagine a post-subject environment for poetic composition informed by post-Anthropocentric time, one which in scale renders null the meaning of metonymic palimpsest through textual reference or the performatives of the necropastoral body.

McSweeney's necropastoral glorifies membranes, diseases, and trenches, like that found in Wilfred Owen's poetry—"Owen escapes from war through a hole eaten in war by war itself ... a saturation which is also a self-evisceration, a digging out—war makes an aperture in war."[15] The most exciting aspect of this project is its overwhelming of membranes and its preference for reanimations that exceed the subject but find some registration within it. Yet, the troubling fact of the Anthropocene and vistas of contamination which pervade it is the knowledge that the eradication of the human species following a climate change eschatology is likely to have the resonant indifference of Gaia to those diseased or displaced registrations in the subject. For humans, the necropasture, for Gaia, the return of Eden. Or, it is better to say that these different iterations of pasture are but limited spheres within the metamorphoses of Gaia. Unlike Rasula's "necropoetics," McSweeney's theory of the necropastoral is less concerned with the threshold thematised between life and death than the flouting of such binaries by outside forces as war or contamination.[16] For me, McSweeney's theory endorses poetic attention to posthuman forces which come to differentiate such concepts, but also contaminate their boundaries.

I discovered both Rasula and McSweeney's theories about the time of the now abandoned *36 Views'* completion. Both poetic critics give an aesthetic as well as ecological orientation to what in the landscape is an enormous, indifferent pastoral will as productive of posthuman futures reorienting human presents. The project's framing is a painterly conceit inspired by Hokusai's epic etchings of thirty-six different views of Mt. Fuji from around Japan, the country in which I live at present and have, now for the second time (first was 2007), since 2015. I have added myself to a line of imitators, including Hokusai's contemporary Hiroshige. The series engaged

---

15 Joyelle McSweeney, "Strange (Political) Meetings in the Necropastoral: Owen, Hawkey, WikiLeaks," in *Montevidayo* (2011), accessed September 10, 2016, http://www.montevidayo.com/?p=941.

16 Rasula, *This Compost*, 64–68.

with an impossibly indifferent pastoralist, Eyjafjallajökull, and its catastrophic eruptions in 2010. Through this event, I came to understand those environments which have become influential, specifically the transpacific environmental difference of Japan, the difference of its earthy soil to the sandy, gravelly places of my rearing in Western Australia. And through all of this until the present, this abandoned series compiles nascent environmental thinking, world ecological event, subjectivity, and my contemporary life in Japan. I now realize that the Pacific Ocean is the primary agent of differentiation. Ocean—what Rasula would call in the context of Whitman's work "the ultimate compost."[17] The Pacific Ocean makes a membrane between my Australian lives and my Japanese ones, the mediator of my ongoing transpacific adventure across a new geological consciousness of ideal landscapes and real ecological indifference to my mind's insubstantial, but substructural, folly.

The volcano, of all things, poses a particular set of problems to the recorder of transpacific experience. The Pacific Ocean's volcanoes, and the tectonics and volcanics which lie beneath it, are formative intensities of this geographical immensity. The volcano is the threshold between what pre-exists the formation of land, and the becoming of land. A volcano is live, a live negotiation and a live and unfinished landmass. A volcano effectively produces its own milieu and sets the terms of fertility in negotiation with contingency, the contingencies of salt and nutriment, the contingencies of water's relation, the contingencies of its later inhabitants. Archipelagos, mountains, and depths, can be traced at some point to the prehistoric events of volcanology. My first important interaction with volcanoes was in 2010, meeting Mt. Usu, or Usuzan, in southern Hokkaido, the north island of Japan, an entity sat on the narrow landmass bordered by the Sea of Japan on one side, and the Pacific Ocean on the other.

The inception of the greater Tōya Caldera sometime around 110,000 BC, of which Usuzan appears at the edge of, opened with an eruption flinging pyroclastic material across all of the north island. The caldera, now filled with water, is the third largest caldera lake in Japan. At its centre sits a tranquil-seeming island called Nakajima, created by activity some 60,000 years later. On the south perimeter of this caldera lake ten kilometres in diameter, more activity, the stratovolcano Usuzan appearing for the first time, this being 20,000 years ago, only to collapse into undulations of hills drifting downwards to the lake approximately 13,000 years later. It's quiet at the site up until three hundred years ago when explicit volcanic activity recommences. The site undergoes the formations of many new craters on a number of occasions between the seventeenth- and nineteenth-centuries. In 1910, presentiments of a far more terrifying century of activity would take place in the shape of a cryptodome—a boil of the earth whose pressure does not yet blow

---

17 Rasula, *This Compost*, 60.

its own top—called Mt. Yosomi, a growth of 117 meters, emerged in *two short months*. Thirty-four years later, a pustule of the earth, the bad omen Showashinzan over the course of one year would sprout from beneath a wheatfield and steam forth to an abominable height of 407 metres at a time when Emperor Hirohito's Japan was recoiling from the Asian continent. This totem would surrender its expansion upwards the very same month the country signed the Japanese Instrument of Surrender in September 1945.[18]

So, does Showashinzan, though emerging in synchrony with dramatic activities of Usuzan in 1945, have anything to do with the later eruptions of Usuzan the parent, hoary and hardly shifting shape but spitting ash and pumice that would drown the local hospital between 1977 and '78? Is the stratovolcanic basin of Tōyako another parent, and our history proceeding just minor incidents? It becomes clear the recordist, and now the poet, scrambles to apprehend and diagrammatise the movements of a volcanic event. The scrambling itself has its own temporality: Masao Mimatsu, a postal officer, became the great and lifelong dilettante volcanologist of Usuzan until his death. Thirdly, in this list of difficulties, is the violence of a volcano. Who can claim they ever recorded the magnitude and tumult of an eruption at the moment of its incipience? In 2010, who observed close enough the eruption at the Eyjafjallajökull massif to see the impending direction of the flood soon to succeed it? Visiting the red mouth of Usuzan and looking down from my minor viewing platform I saw only a clean erosion of earth, revealing a set of strata rings, like that revealed by the slicing of a gum tree's boll. It was as if at its hell mouth the volcano could reveal its true temporality, the temporality enacted at the event's centre, the inapprehensible movement of liquid becoming land. I was witness to no eruption, just Usuzan biding its time, smoking indifferently. If Hokkaido's pastures and their fertility were born from volcanic becoming, the atemporal material intensity of Gaia itself, then the status of landscape and of experience was immediately called into question. Writing as a form of memorialisation would have to, I thought, consider palimpsest, textual specimen, and necropasture alike as phenomena unfixed in time to grapple with Usuzan's history. The Pacific Ocean, the house of the Ring of Fire, became a broader connection between worlds I had once felt to be divided, predicated as they were by the force of geography and geology.

Geophysicists may have an empirical task, but their insights necessitate a negotiation with this atemporal indifference to the human. They can tell us just how old Usuzan is without having to uncover the vellum manuscript of another Masao Mimatsu. They can approximate the startling antiquity of the Bungle Bungles in the Kimberley in Australia. Soil, at least, lends itself better to the guessing hands

---

18 For more information on Showashinzan and Usuzan in Southern Hokkaido in Japan, visit this comprehensive website on geophysical activities at the site: http://www.toya-usu-geopark.org/en.

and eyes of a poet who takes as material what is most immediately obvious. Being an Australian and moving to Japan for a year in 2007, one environmental difference was staggering to me between the two countries, far removed from the cultural clichés. I say countries, however this observation has more to do with a distinction between Perth, on the south-west coast of Western Australia, and the central Kanto region of Japan within which Tokyo sits. In the empty lot behind my apartment block in Oizumi-machi on the flatlands of Gunma-ken the earth was as black as potting mix. It seemed so nutritious it seemed artificial. Returning to Australia in 2008, suddenly the gravelly, light-brown soil and the sands of the northern suburbs of Perth seemed absurdly formidable. Usuzan, later, would explain this all to me, that my time served with different earths was also, in another sense, the navigation of the records of different geological times, all mediated, transpacifically, by a massive oceanic divide. In Japan, the found objects of treks were missing, like West Australia's granite, its petrifying honkey nuts, and its whole spheres of the red-brown gravel that fills every expanse of earth in the Darling Ranges, where I lived from two to eighteen years of age. Showashinzan's multi-coloured pate, by constrast, shimmers and burns with an undefined, magmatic time, from which who knows what compost and what floral subjects will emerge after the violence of its emergence.

Australia, the first place I ever called home, vibrates at a different tectonic pitch and remembers its volcanic prehistory with a wider historical berth. Thus, the fertile mind on this other hemisphere of the Pacific engages with geological potentiality differently. Fertility in the hands of Australian poet John Kinsella, for example, is conceptually at odds with the foolish pastoralism imported by the British colonizers of the Australian continent. In *Salt*, a collaborative book with prose writer Robert Drewe, fertility appears in glimpses on the surface of deep history, appearing in the guile of the salt-tolerant samphire, for example, calling home the ecosystem of the desert. An Australian poetics of Pacific difference might be forged somewhere between contemporary Aboriginal Australian poet Lionel Fogarty's poem "Biral Biral" and its consciousness of the volcanic history of geology: "Mountains lazy survived future dispensed / cause land [...],"[19] its tellingly conflicted tenses on the status of a mountain's productions, and John Kinsella's poem "Geraldton": "and sand rolling in heaps, / shaped and reshaped and held down / by a scrub defying / rules of fertility, / the ocean breathing life into the green succulence, / the sun doing the rest."[20] The sun is progenitor, the ocean is promulgator, and succulence is the symbol, in one respect. For Kinsella, "scrub" defies "rules of fertility," the Australian scrub recomposing the very question of fertility. One imagines it must

---

19 Lionel G. Fogarty, *New and Selected Poems: munaldjali, mutuerjaraera* (South Melbourne: Hyland House, 1995), 88.
20 John Kinsella and Robert Drewe, *Sand* (Fremantle: Fremantle Arts Press, 2010), 175.

have been as transgressive an image to European sensibilities of fertility for the first European to arid Australia who would be baffled to find a grass so hardy rushing upwards, greenly, from sand. For me, as it is for Kinsella, fertility and the mind which interrogates it are inevitably hermeneutic, a taxonomy which ecology continually redefines the terms upon which it is interpreted. The volcanoes of Hokkaido, as well as the dunes of Western Australia, propose an incendiary and violent fertility that pose great affronts to the extractive Divinity-sucking of which Thomas Browne speaks, and a greater manifold of potential than our plots of temporarily fertile land dreamt in our pastoralisms. Under these resonate other forces, and other times, under which might we find other minds.

I conclude with a picture from the time of these ideas' convergence, the poem "The Bad Omen Showashinzan." This poem from 2011 is my record of this convergence, gathering poets, facts, sensations, concepts, and philosophies still eructating, morphing, curdling, but no doubt, like Showashinzan, taking an unrecognisable appearance within present landscapes. The poem returns this reader, at least, to a cyclonic memorial to transpacific earth underfoot.

THE BAD OMEN SHOWASHINZAN

Usuzan's abeyance belated mourning.
Depressed by a presentation of an end come red
then blue, the exhibition of a smoking cranium.
Chairlift of hairs.
The people are shifting for four years, then forty,
then a million! Their hands at once digging the crust
then boiling, then refreshing the flesh boilers to recovery.
The eruption began as a flare on the 28th of December 1943,
ejecting the young windbreak of poplars
bordering the wheatfields in January,
only to evict everything in June.

Now the hairs collaborate for ownership of the ropeway,
relic to the industrial romance of absence.

A cease-and-desist measure at the time of transcendental no-surrender.
No reply at genius hill. A canary congratulates the feedback loop.

We are no longer a fleet of crows, we are marauding vermin, say humans.
If we do not kill you, the putrefaction of our bowels will poison you eventually.

The carbuncle as round as the Firenze Duomo
and as tall, as red as a fleeing sun, as hot as failure,
pustule becomes a mountain. Locals of Tōya! Have your spades melted?
Where are the journalisms?

Geology sizzles. Missives crave absent wheat uncalculated.
Usuzan's sibilance mirror coughs on eructation memorial.
Yōtei can't move for Fuji, its hectares of gravelled earth.
The high-vis labourers are abseiling, I think. Their clocks are wet.

It is minus six degrees and makes everything the likeness of a cadaver,
a ruse to write journals by. We steam eggs over cracks in loam and crust.
All else is dead but shreds of grass, but the grass sprints. It's green so quick
the black softens.

Sunset makes a farewell flare
in the memory of apparitional vests.

BIBLIOGRAPHY

Deleuze, Gilles. *The Logic of Sense*. Translated by Mark Lester. London: Continuum, 2009.

Fogarty, Lionel G. *New and Selected Poems: munaldjali, mutuerjaraera*. South Melbourne: Hyland House, 1995), 88.

Kinsella, John, and Robert Drewe. *Sand*. Fremantle: Fremantle Arts Press, 2010.

Latour, Bruno. "An Attempt at a 'Compositionist' Manifesto." *New Literary History* 41 (2010): 471–490.

McSweeney, Joyelle. "Garbage In/Garbage In the Necropastoral: On the Road to Kimp'o Landfill: Kim Hyesoon & Camile Rose Garcia & Césaire." *Montevidayo* (2011), accessed September 10, 2016. http://www.montevidayo.com/?p=1255#more-1255.

--. "Necropastoral, or, Normal Love." *Montevidayo* (2011), accessed September 10, 2016. http://www.montevidayo.com/?p=788.

--. *The Necropastoral: Poetry, Media, Occults*. Ann Arbor: University of Michigan Press, 2014.

--. "Strange (Political) Meetings in the Necropastoral: Owen, Hawkey, WikiLeaks." *Montevidayo* (2011), accessed September 10, 2016. http://www.montevidayo.com/?p=941.

Rasula, Jed. *This Compost: Ecological Imperative in American Poetry*. Athens: University of Georgia Press, 2002.

--. and Steve McCaffery, eds. *Imagining Language: An Anthology*. Cambridge, Massachusetts and London, England: The MIT Press, 1998.

Whitman, Walt. *Specimen Days & Collect*. New York: Dover Publications, 1995.

Wordsworth, William. "Preface to Lyrical Ballads, with Pastoral and Other Poems (1802)." In *The Norton Anthology of English Literature: The Romantic Period*, edited by Stephen Greenblatt. New York: W.W. Norton & Company, 2006.

FROM *A BELL MADE OF STONES*

LEHUA M. TAITANO

iknewaboyonce
whowasmissing
aneye.thesee-
ingonewasthe
colorofkelp,
thefalseone
algae.hewas
lovedbyallfor
hismarksman's
skill(aflight-
lessbirdatone-
hundredpaces,
squarebetween)
thoughirecall
mosthiscasual
useof"half-breed"
inenglishclass
adaywhenthe
radiatorsstank
ofpiss,hissing.
iwascounting
cardinalsonthe
limb,enoughto
formawound..

asamplingfromtheguamvisitorsbureau.
theisland: 6,000milesfromsanfrancisco
3,800mileswestofhonolulu
1,500milessouthofjapan
wascreatedfrompeaksoftwoancientvolcanoes
thatsankintothesea
(Agana)
population: canbedividedintothreeethnicgroups
originalinhabitantsmakeup
approximately37%
politicalstatus: one(1)non-votingcongressional
delegatetothehouseofrepresentatives
history: bycanoe
clanandcaste
matrilineal
isolatedfromtherestofthe world
magellan
broughtcatholicismandawesternway
newera
japaneseforcesassumedcontrol
u.s.troopsreclaimed
organic.
gettingthere: gateways
accommodations: regionalhotelchainshavebeachfront
language: englishandchamorro
climate: providingexcellentopportunitiesforwatersports
attractions: petroglyphs
lattestones(pillars)
spanishruins
wwiimemorials
totransformdishesintoachamorromeal,
requestfinadene
abitofanytsauce
usually,familystylefinadenehasmoreheat
traveldocuments (entryandexitformalities):
citizens
of
most other
countries
musthave
avalid
passport

mynananbiha,beforedying.
soonitishappening,shesays.
(shesitsonanoverturnedbucketintheshadeoftheconcretehouse)
soonitishappening.
(blotchyswollenlegscataracteyesthebendofbreadfruittrees)
ai'adai,shesays.whowilltakecareofmyflowers?
(hibiscusbigasplatesBougainvilleaatumbleofheartbursts)
shesays,forheaven'sgracious.thesunisbleedingintothesea.

below.
taketheglobeandspinitslowlyinyourhands
beneaththehardequatoriallinethereisalittle
stringofislands.marianas. (praisemary)
probewithpointedfingerandpronounceitaloud.
theflecksspittlethatescapesyourlips
cornerwillfallonguahan
                                (youknowitasguam)
theworldwasmadebysiblings
brothersister
brothersister
brother'sdyingbreathbecamethesky.
brother'sevestheshadowmoon.
theworldwasmadebysiblings
sistergatheredbrother'sbackinherhands
andformedthespineoftheearth.
brother'sflowinghairbecamethesea.
sisterbrother
sisterbrother
ofcourse,sister'sbodyhardenedtostone.
wavescrashwavescrashwavescrashwavesandwaves
crashintoher.pieceschippedawaybecame
the
peopleofguahan.theworldmadebysiblings.
brothersistersubterranean.sisterbrothersub
terranean
guahan-cum-guam-cum-guahanisthepuncturing
tip
ofamountainrestingsuboceana.
theauroraresortvilla andspawasbuiltonguahanguam
ontopofskeletons.brotherssistersdatingfrom4000.c.
theyhavebeenexhumed.boxed.shipped (praisemary)
awaitingclassification.

nationalarchivesandrecordsadministration.
frequentlyaskedquestions:
cancitizensinu.s.territories
voteforpresident?
no.theelectoralcollegesystem
doesnotprovidefor...
unlesscitizensinu.s.territories
haveofficialresidency(domicile)
inau.s.state...
notethatpriortotheadoptionofthe
twenty-thirdamendment,d.c.residents
couldnotvoteinthepresidential
election.

          un-inc.

       mymotherflashesafoottattoo,
       asinglepenpricked
                        dotgonegreen
                            gray.
       i'dliketothink
       shehatesthemarkthoughi've
       neverknownhertohate. theboy,
       letlooseapen,planteditthere,
       backinaschoolroomwhere
       herlanguagewasdenied   where
       englishwasfavored
       whitegrammar.(theamericankind)
       shelearnedtounlearnherkind.
       the
          Chamoruboy
                    hasaspanishname
                 (praisemary)
       he letlooseafountain
       pen
          duringexercisesinobjectivity
       asin
           iversusyou

       in
         irecognizeyou.
       reversed,theimpliedisthesame
                   (unspokenyou).
       accidentalsshesays.
       itlandedtrue. the
       pentipaperfectprick
                        sunkdeeplikea

       flagpole.
       shewaswearingnoshoesshe
       walkswiththatfootonthemainland
       farfrom
                        theisland

       asmallmoleoftattoointhesea
       ofherbrownfootskinpenningaplace.
       theboy'sname
                   floresorcruz.

NON-LOCAL LOCALITIES:
TRANS-PACIFIC CONNECTIONS BETWEEN
ABORIGINAL AND MAPUCHE POETRY

STUART COOKE

"Home" is not a bounded, strictly measureable area, but something porous and open to visitors. It consists of territory that might be fought for, but it does not fit neatly within the lines on a map. Depending on the needs at hand, the home may change. Indeed, at different times and places, one could talk about the entire planet as "home." In this sense, "home" constitutes the *absolute space* available for habitation: a borderless region, or what Gilles Deleuze and Félix Guattari call a "nonlimited locality." But to think in terms of the absolute does not require that we always think globally (as if we were conquistadors looking at the planet from space); rather, the absolute is achieved "in an infinite succession of local operations" at ground level.[1]

Understanding such "local operations" in an absolute sense can form the basis of a relationship between Mapuche and Aboriginal poetics. Rather than neglecting their specificities beneath an abstracted notion of a "global indigenous poetics," poets like Paulo Huirimilla and Lionel Fogarty can communicate with one another precisely because of their commitment to the open systems of their *locations*.

Born on the island of Calbuco (south of Puerto Montt) in 1974, Paulo Huirimilla identifies as Huilliche-Mapuche.[2] His paternal grandparents came from the nearby islands of Chaulinec and Puluqui, and his maternal grandparents from Quigua Island, which are all located in the Archipelago of the Chonos (south of the large island of Chiloé). In the mid-nineties he moved to the southern town of Osorno (in between Valdivia and Puerto Montt), where he undertook studies in Spanish and Latin American literature. Since 2006 he has been living with his wife and son in Puerto Montt, where he works as a high school teacher and as a teacher of Mapuzugun, the main language of the Mapuche people. Huirimilla's *Palimpsesto* [Palimpsest] (2005) was declared by critic and scholar Hugo Carrasco to be one of

---

1 Gilles Deleuze and Félix Guattari, *A Thousand Plateaus: Capitalism and Schizophrenia*, trans. Brian Massumi (London & New York: Continuum, 2004), 422.
2 The term *Huilliche* doesn't refer to an ethnic domination, but rather a geographical one. Their territory, known as *Huichan Mapu* ("great land of the south"), corresponds to the tenth region of Chile, which extends from Valdivia to Chiloé. Within this region lies a further distribution of smaller groups.

the most significant books in recent years by a Mapuche writer.[3] In 2008 Huirimilla travelled to Australia with another Mapuche poet, Roxana Miranda Rupailaf; the journey would lead to the writing of "Ríos de Cisnes" [Rivers of Swans], included and translated in full at the end of this essay.

It is relatively easy to identify North American and European influences in much of Huirimilla's work, but "Ríos de Cisnes" suggests the beginnings of an entirely different literary relationship. A dramatic poem of ten parts, "Ríos de Cisnes" is notable both as the *ars poetica* of a contemporary Mapuche poet and as an attempt to expand Mapuche consciousness far beyond the South American cone. The central image of the red-crested swan is a symbol of an Australian-Chilean geography, emblematic of the black-necked and completely black swans found in Chile and Australia respectively; of even more interest is the way in which the poem actively seeks out this trans-Pacific connection.

From the outset of "Ríos de Cisnes," the birds are swans-becoming-text:

The river of swans sprays foam
On the ocean of the white page,
Searching for the red crest and black neck
In the signs of the *lamilla*.

Physical and textual worlds are merged here; indeed, text can be found within the world itself, in the signs of *la lamilla*, a coffee-coloured seaweed eaten by the swans. As text, then, the swans leave the confines of their physical bodies to travel within the signs on the page. However, the birds are suffering: they "can sell their vegetables no longer" because the waters they use to irrigate their crops have become contaminated with heavy metals. The conflation of human agricultural activity with the lives of the swans signals an important point about the swans' home-place: it is no longer sustainable. For the poem to continue, therefore, the swans must expand their localities and search for other lands. That is, if poetic language is to continue to survive as an expression of the physical world, this world must be vibrant and healthy. For the Mapuche, the notion of biodiversity or, in Mapuzugun, *Icrofil Mogen* (which roughly translates as "the complete world"), is not limited purely to conceptions of the natural or non-human order. Instead, like Guattari's concept of "the three ecologies," *Icrofil Mogen* also involves social and cultural dimensions, since the human is *of* the earth in Mapuche thought.[4] When culture is deemed part of nature, in other words, the focus is not on "Nature," but on how "[the language of] Culture" is a sign of the health of the biosphere.

---

3 Mabel García, Hugo Carrasco, and Verónica Contreras, *Crítica situada: el estado actual del arte y la poesía Mapuche* (Temuco: Universidad de la Frontera, 2005), 79.
4 Elicura Chihuailaf, *Recado confidencial a los chilenos* (Santiago: LOM, 1999), 52.

This point is emphasised later on in the poem, when we come across the ghostly figure of Gabriela Mistral. We see that the Nobel laureate is singing to the remaining birds, so few of whom remain because the others have "been displaced by law and rifle" as pressures on the ecosystem have increased. The direction of the poet's song towards these few remnants of a once flourishing colony is telling: Mistral is singing in "the language of ... the world"; all that she sings of, then, must be *in* this world; without a world, there is nothing to sing about. The world provides the poet with the language for her song. If we attempt to retreat to an abstracted realm of signification, the sign of the swan will still appear, "but without meaning." For meaning must come from the way that language is an expression of world. Here we return to the conception of language as Mapuzugun, or the language of the earth. However, where an older Mapuche poet like Elicura Chihuailaf might romanticise poetic language as "the song that is necessary in order to live with ourselves and with others,"[5] Huirimilla—while not disagreeing with the notion—is arguing that if these "others" are not healthy and flourishing, there can be *no language* to begin with.

In the quest to diversify and grow more resilient, Huirimilla has decided that *all* language and meaning-making is of the earth. In doing so, he is not asking that language deny the local but, on the contrary, that we never forget its attachment to the local. Thus, we read in the seventh part of the poem, when he is carrying a swan on his shoulder, that the swan is:

> [...] a *Pingangu*
> Colour albino
> *Mutro* we say

The swan is identified in Mapuzugun, then we read of its golden, "albino" colour, which in turn is translated as *mutro*. The phrase "we say" immediately associates the speaker with a community of the Mapuche people. The general movement, however, is one of translation—from Mapuzugun (*Pingangu*) to Spanish (to English) and back to Mapuzugun again (*mutro*). Although no place of rest exists in any one language, and the poet needs to keep shifting among many, he doesn't discard the importance of the swans' home, or its importance to his poetry. To protect his locale, however, the poet has opened it to engagement with others.

Accordingly, in the eighth part of the poem we arrive at a dramatic climax, in which the speaker has arrived in a new land:

> I turn around in the island desert like the black swan with red crest.
> I fly around looking for the inland sea.
> I have seen it in these other black swans with red crests.

---

5 Ibid., 69.

These "other black swans" are "the Koori swans," the Indigenous Australians of whom Huirimilla became aware when he visited the "island desert" in 2008. He sings for their "rainbow snakes" and hopes that these snakes will "breathe eternally against oblivion."[6] In a remarkable passage, Huirimilla seemingly stumbles upon a virtual realm replete with connective possibilities, in which dance, music and art converge to produce a powerful synergy of trans-Pacific histories:

> I see one dance and sing the way her grandmother did
> and the grandmother of her grandmothers
> and she paints a white fabric with many spots of colour
> which become the parallel dreams of my kidnapped grandparents
> who speak through my saliva.
> [...]
> May you swim now, Koori swans with all your rainbow snakes ...[7]

The poem then crosses to the banks of the Thames in London in yet another international leap before we find, in the subsequent and final part, that the swans have formed pairs. In a show of solidarity, the pairs of "the black necks walk on the ocean" between Chile and Australia. Importantly, these swans appear to the speaker "on another island / On a page." The *page* is the source of potential for cross-Pacific partnership; its smooth, white space is the event horizon between the virtual realm of the future and the present. For Huirimilla the page "is more luminous than rebellion," suggesting that its translations of potential—from places, animals and people into moments of poetic language—are the most important sources of cultural strength. Yet this bi-national vision of Huirimilla's does not involve his ascent to an outlook *above* both territories. Rather, he remains in Southern Chile, where he calls to the swans "from the beach of the petrified cypress ... through the air choked with fumes and ash." In this semi-apocalyptic landscape he still finds hope, but in order for this hope to be actualised he would need help from the other side of the Pacific Ocean.

Some of Huirimilla's poems appeared relatively recently in the first bi-lingual Aboriginal and Mapuche anthology of art and poetry.[8] In years to come, this anthology might produce further potential for cross-Pacific relationships; for now,

---

6   There are intriguing similarities between the rainbow serpents of many Aboriginal Dreaming stories and those two Mapuche creation serpents, Kai-Kai and Tren-Tren. Primarily, both Mapuche and Aboriginal serpents gave the land its current form by moving through it.

7   "Koori" is the term used by Aboriginal people from parts of New South Wales and Victoria to refer to themselves.

8   Gonzalo Rojas and Peter Minter, eds., *Espejo de tierra (Earth Mirror)* (Canberra: Chilean Embassy, 2008).

however, it is in Murri poet Lionel Fogarty's work that we see the strongest example in Aboriginal literature of commitment to an international fight for indigenous peoples' justice.[9] For many years, Fogarty has been urging his people to "fight / like the red man has done,"[10] drawing particular strength and inspiration from North American developments in indigenous rights and poetics. Born in 1958 at Barambah Mission in southeastern Queensland (now known as Cherbourg Aboriginal Reserve),[11] Fogarty is of the Yoogum and Kudjela tribes. Since his activist role in the liberation movements of the '70s (highlighted, perhaps, by his address to the American Indian Movement of the Second International Indian Treaty Council in the USA in 1976), Fogarty has always seen the struggle for land rights in relation to the struggles of indigenous peoples globally.[12] In the nationalist climate of "Australian poetry," dominated by the English language and by variations of confessional, lyric poetry, Fogarty's poems are often extremely confronting. For Philip Mead, they present "difficult and unresolved questions about the relation between language, nation and identity [...] in the face of powerful interests that want to settle the question of identity and language, literally, once and for all, to act as though it was settled from the beginning."[13]

Much of Fogarty's poetry has an undeniably international flavour, particularly *Minyung Woolah Binnung (What Saying Says)*, some of which is informed by contact with Latin America. The first poem in the book, "Balance Earth 20057 Corroborate Love," a call for a global gathering of lovers, is soon followed by a poem called "Embassy."[14] "Embassy" is about the shocks to thought that can take place during a period of international travel, leading to the development of new intellectual pathways and social networks:

Travelling in another lands people
    sparkling thoughts struck minds

Later in the book a peculiar moment occurs in "I Sus I,"[15] in which Fogarty appears to write the opening words in Spanish, before continuing the poem without any

---

9   *Murri* is the term used by Aboriginal people from Queensland to refer to themselves.

10 From Lionel Fogarty, "For I Come—Death in Custody" in *Macquarie PEN Anthology of Aboriginal Literature*, eds. Anita Heiss and Peter Minter (Sydney: Allen & Unwin, 2008), 92.

11 Throughout the twentieth century, Aboriginal people from many disparate tribal groups were forcibly removed to Cherbourg, which became the largest settlement of its kind in Queensland.

12 Philip Mead, *Networked Language: culture & history in Australian poetry* (North Melbourne: Australian Scholarly Publishing, 2008), 425.

13 Ibid., 403.

14 Lionel Fogarty, *Minyung Woolah Binnung (What Saying Says): poems and drawings* (Southport: Keeaira Press, 2004), 12–14.

15 Ibid., 22.

further reference to them. The first two words of the line "Dos messes Intrinsic" are too close to a phonetic transcription of the Spanish *dos meses* [two months] to go unnoticed, but at the same time there is no other use of the language anywhere else in the book. Then, "Bina Open Hearts Precedents" is for the refugees of the civil war in El Salvador, while "Ningla-a-na" is, as we will soon see, a bold attempt to link Latin American and Australian histories of colonisation.

Mirroring Huirimilla's own trans-nationalism, Fogarty's response to the plight of Chile's indigenous peoples proposes a relationship between language and identity that is *not* mediated by ideas of nation, or even of ethnicity. Rather, in the eyes of these two poets, what unites indigenous peoples from Latin America and Australia is shared histories of resistance to territorial dispossession, where "territory" is a central and pervasive agency. Their peoples' similarities, in other words, are to do with their responsibilities for their localities. Their parallel histories then bring these localities into contact, expanding them. By virtue of such expansion, for Huirimilla and Fogarty the local has become *nonlimited*. Land, in this sense, becomes a proper noun:

we must unite on Land we relate to better than rich[16]

It is central to their poetry that both of these poets speak *from* their land, rather than from a transcendent plane *above* it. For this reason Fogarty writes of "our indigenous brother and sisters over there" in the poem "Ningla-a-na":[17] they are "over there" because the poet is "here," fighting for his own country that gives him and his people "all / laws and security to pass on."

Then, in a recent poem, "Mapuche 'Campesinos,'"[18] Fogarty is completely explicit about the brother- and sister-hood he feels with the Mapuche. "I'm glad you are to reclaim land," he writes, and then:

Live on, we are the earth the land
Indigenous Chilean you shall shine in our heart's spirits

Mapuche might baulk at being called "Indigenous Chileans" ("No somos Chilenos," many will tell you, "somos *Mapuche*!") but the more pertinent point is that Fogarty doesn't seem to be aware of this. He is speaking a *local* discourse rather than an international one, in which his language is very firmly attached to the realities of Murri life. Grounded in his local context, he calls on Native Americans:

---

16 From "Mapuche 'Campesinos,'" in Lionel Fogarty, Yvette Walker, and Kargun Fogarty, *Yerrabilela Jimbelung: poems about friends and family* (Southport: Keeaira Press, 2008), 53.

17 Fogarty, *Minyung Woolah Binnung*, 58–9.

18 Fogarty, Walker, and Fogarty, *Yerrabilela Jimbelung*, 53.

it's now we must build an indigenous
international communists united force
to have liberation here we natives
have to collect our culture

The mention of communism here may lead us to make vague associations with Latin American communist writers like Pablo Neruda. Where Neruda rose up to assume the voice of Indigenous America in *Las Alturas de Macchu Picchu*, however, Fogarty insists on speaking as part of a much larger population:

Maybe we been see over the Americas
so aborigines bring back our guerrilla fighter
Che Guevara well armed in action
inter out well-known Pan Aboriginalism
struggles Argentina 'gumboo' we shall 'attack'
naturally lead by our old spearheading

Clearly, the Americas are always "over there" for Fogarty, as opposed to "down there" or "right there." The first-person is absent from much of his work; as one of many, he is speaking from an immanent place rather than a transcendent one. Indeed, the final line of "Ningla-a-na" might serve as a corrective for the "dead mouths" of which Neruda famously sung in the aforementioned poem. "[W]e are hungry for our lands," Fogarty writes. That is, "*we* are hungry for our lands," where hunger signifies a desire to *eat*, and eating is done by open, and living, mouths. No less important, either, is the fact that "we" are speaking, and shedding the imposed settlement of silence.

Here we come to see why Bridie McCarthy concluded, in her pioneering thesis on Latin American and Australian poetry, that an engagement with Latin American poetry might show how Australian poetry is *already* amenable to transnational networks of communication. Shared colonial politics of genocide and dispossession across the Pacific can contribute to a synergetic power in the poetics, which isn't weakened necessarily by divergent histories, or by differing forms of colonisation.[19] This responds to Mead's call that we imagine "Australian literature" not as a national canon, but as a network of discourses in which we can read a series of relational practices "exceeding and resisting all culturally nationalist definitions and priorities."[20] In an interview with Mead some years ago, Fogarty himself noted that

---

19 Bridie McCarthy, "At the Limits: postcolonial and hyperreal translations of Australian poetry" (PhD Thesis, Deakin University, 2006), 208 and 210.
20 Mead, *Networked Language*, 401.

I'd really like to get all my poetry overseas and I'd like to get it to places in Europe, in Asia, in America, and the Pacific. I mean I'd like to get it to communities of indigenous people as well as into bourgeois society ... [21]

So it is no doubt the case that Fogarty has long been predisposed to figure his work in a variety of national and international contexts. He wants his poems to create "a collective thought within people so that they can go back and read other Aboriginal literature or whiteman's literature [which] will help them to meditate, so that they can create an energy, good energy."[22] This good, creative energy is the imagination of a cohesive, postcolonial environment, at once democratic and inclusive in its scope, and stridently expansive in its willingness to relate to other, like-minded environments. He wants the reading of his poetry to produce, in a very real and literal sense, a Deleuzian "deterritorialisation" of previously foreign territories. Read together, then, poems like "Ríos de Cisnes" and "Mapuche 'Campesinos'" constitute a kind of becoming. They perform, to paraphrase Brian Massumi, "an operation on ... group-policed categories of thought and action." Such a reading experience "opens a space in the grid of identities those categories delineate, inventing new trajectories, [...] unheard-of futures and possible bodies such as have never been seen before."[23]

In order to continue to resist capture and containment, the poem needs to avoid becoming rooted in any one particular place or identity, releasing itself from such borders to become "light or deterritorialized."[24] The poems don't become so light as to float *away*; rather, their poetry always needs to be in touch with the ground, with the forces responsible for life. For indigenous poets like Fogarty and Huirimilla, the goal is a constant redefinition of the conditions of existence laid down by the dominant, cultural order; they want to convert these accepted conditions into conditions of becoming: "The end is for there to be no end."[25] To paraphrase poet and theorist Charles Bernstein, Fogarty and Huirimilla might be bringing together distinct cultural groups, and making problematic their national affiliations in the process, in order "to forge new collective identities that will enable a more resourceful resistance to rigidly territorializing clannishness and paralysing depoliticizing codicity."[26] This new collectivity is why, in poems like "Ríos de

---

21 Lionel Fogarty and Philip Mead, "Lionel Fogarty in Conversation with Philip Mead," http://jacketmagazine.com/01/fogartyiv.html.

22 Ibid.

23 Brian Massumi, *A User's Guide to Capitalism and Schizophrenia: deviations from Deleuze and Guattari*, 1996 ed. (Cambridge, Mass.: MIT Press, 1992), 101.

24 Paraphrasing John Rajchman, *The Deleuze Connections* (Cambridge & London: MIT Press, 2000), 95.

25 Massumi, *A User's Guide to Capitalism and Schizophrenia*, 104.

26 Charles Bernstein, "Poetics of the Americas," *Modernism/Modernity* 3, no. 3 (1996), 19.

Cisnes," "Mapuche 'Campesinos'" and "Ningla-a-na," the conclusion of each poem is written in the present tense: the lines depict actions in progress, which will continue long after the poem itself has ended:

myself I call them from the beach of the petrified cypress

we are hungry for our lands

Chile Mapuche we are with you to liberation

That remarkable eighth part of "Ríos de Cisnes," in which Huirimilla sees in the paintings of the Koori people "the parallel dreams of my kidnapped grandparents," is the envisioning of a kind of virtual realm, or the possibility of a reality which has not yet attained a physical actuality, but instead resides only in the realm of imagination. Fogarty, in both "Mapuche 'Campesinos'" and "Ningla-a-na," explores precisely the same kind of virtuality. In the former of these poems, it emerges as the poem's startling conclusion:

We had civilization before they came so us know the way to a future
Chile Mapuche we are with you to liberation

In the latter, the vision is yet hazier and more ill-defined:

500 years ahead we will be survive in
off our lands overseas

Here, as much as the concept of liberation itself is still in the realm of the virtual, Fogarty's disregard for traditional structures of English grammar allows the forms of his visions to echo something of the fluidity of their content. Writing in a "conventional literary language" would reflect a willingness to abide by the linguistic and epistemological norms of a culture and to negotiate with these norms. For Bernstein, writing in Standard English instead of a more overtly hybrid mode riddled with fissures and ruptures would "obliterate or overcome such marks of difference."[27]

Both Fogarty and Huirimilla write in languages that are quite distinct from their "Standard" English or Spanish counterparts. Such exploratory writing does not escape from its sociohistorical location but rather, according to Bernstein, "contributes to an interrogation and reformulation of the *description* of that sociohistorical situation." Bernstein is writing here about a "poetics of the

---

27 Ibid., 11.

Americas"—a writing necessarily multi-lingual and -national, aspects of which we would need to apply to a trans-Pacific indigenous poetics, too. A poetics of the Americas is about "foregrounding heterogeneous and anomalous elements rather than homogenizing ones." This Bernstein contrasts with nationalist "attempts to represent an already constituted idea of identity [that] may preclude the possibility of encountering *newly emerging identity formations*" [my emphasis].[28] As a progressive politics, however, this poses a distinct problem, because "[n]o Party, no group of intellectuals, can ever fully represent or direct such 'movements,' such 'becomings.'" The relation of the intellectual, artist or poet to such a movement, therefore, must change "from a 'representational' to an 'experimental' role" in order to free the social imagination from preconceived images or representations. So the poet becomes "part of the 'fabulation of a people to come,'" which, because it is "no longer tied to the 'imagined communities of a time or place,'" would contrast markedly with myths about original or past peoples.[29]

As for a poetics of the Americas, an experimental imagination is crucial for any trans-Pacific poetics, too. In poems like "Ecology" and "Ríos de Cisnes" an experimental approach to reality allows for lateral transfers of matter and energy to take place across organisms. Such lateral transference is a kind of neoevolutionism, where movement occurs not primarily by hierarchical productions (as in traditional, Darwinian conceptions of evolution), but also "by transversal communications between heterogeneous populations."[30] This is another crucial characteristic of becoming: it occurs like a rhizome across categories, not along genealogical or classificatory trees. Indeed, after three billion years, writes theoretical physicist Freeman Dyson, lateral, cultural evolution has become the main driving force of change:

> Cultural evolution is not Darwinian. Cultures spread by horizontal transfer of ideas more than by genetic inheritance. Cultural evolution is running a thousand times faster than Darwinian evolution, taking us into a new era of cultural interdependence which we call globalisation.[31]

The task for Aboriginal and Mapuche poets like Fogarty and Huirimilla is to ensure that this horizontal transfer of culture never ceases to take place—that the world never solidifies in a new, albeit "globalised," state.

Horizontal transfer is much faster than rigid, hierarchical patterns of change, allowing huge amounts of information to be transferred freely across strains and

---

28 Ibid., 1.
29 Rajchman, *The Deleuze Connections*, 101.
30 Deleuze and Guattari, *Thousand Plateaus: Capitalism and Schizophrenia*, 263.
31 Freeman Dyson, "Our Biotech Future," http://www.nybooks.com/articles/20370.

even species. In both political and ecological senses, a hierarchical approach to change weakens systems, leaving them more vulnerable to consumption by fast-moving, horizontal evolutions. Allowing information to interact freely and laterally promotes a flow of energy and heterogeneity demanded by the intensities of the situations at hand. Such high-speed reactions can produce tremendous resilience over relatively short spans of time.[32] In this sense, the rapid transference of cultural replicators across national borders, what Dyson calls globalisation, can develop a potent resistance to the ponderous, though powerful, discourses of nationalist institutions. In terms of poetics, what we can see in these poems by Fogarty and Huirimilla is an attempt to "horizontally" develop their own kind of resilience to state-sponsored forms of hierarchical control and exploitation. Such is the value of a more-than-local indigenous poetics.

However, this trans-national poetics raises important questions to do with the variety of attractors that drive one towards the moment of poetic expression. When Fogarty begins a poem, "Chile our liberation fight is the same / Indigenous courage we must unite on Land we relate to better than rich" ("Mapuche 'Campesinos'"), he is responding in a local way to issues which are necessarily more-than-local. It is also the case that Huirimilla felt drawn to make a sort of global statement about events in southern Chile in "Ríos de Cisnes." These articulations span areas far beyond the original localities of the poets, suggesting that there is an impersonal expressive agency abroad *throughout* the world—one that is not fundamentally subjective, nor restricted even to a particular place or language, but which flows freely across subjects. This is a Deleuzian conception of expression: "abroad in the world ... non-local, scattered across myriad struggles ... "[33] Similar to organisms, which are, in a simplified manner of talking, "resilient patterns" in a turbulent flow of energy,[34] bodies are resilient complexes that expression uses like conduits, adopting each one for its temporary articulation. This is expression's own "turbulent flow": it is "always on the move, always engrossed in its own course, over-spilling individual experience, nomadically evading responsibility."[35] Expression moves laterally across ecologies.

---

32 Manuel de Landa, *A Thousand Years of Nonlinear History*, 2003 ed. (New York: Zone Books, 1997), 175. For example, this explains why, since its introduction in 1941, a majority of penicillin's targets (staphylococci) have become resistant to it. Today, nearly every disease known to medicine has become resistant to at least one antibiotic, producing what de Landa terms an "arms race" between hierarchical medical institutions and a "rapidly evolving meshwork of microbes."

33 Brian Massumi, "Introduction: like a thought," in *A Shock to Thought: Expression after Deleuze and Guattari* (London & New York: Routledge, 2002), xxi.

34 Carl R. Woese, "A New Biology for a New Century," *Microbiology and Molecular Biology Reviews* 68, no. 2 (2004): 176.

35 Massumi, "Introduction: Like a thought," xxi.

To understand the relation of the local and the global in this sense obviously requires a particular openness. The poetics must remain forever conjectural and presuppose no stability of ideology or form, for to do so would result in a failed attempt to trap expression within a closed structure. Syntax cannot make bold suppositions or conclusions, therefore, and statements about the world must be sensitive to the world's own resistance to definition. Consequently, a trans-Pacific poetics must be less replete with realistic details than a more descriptive or analogical poetics, which clings to the local so tightly that it allows no sense of the local's capacity for change. Because free, indirect discourse is the basis of all language, a trans-Pacific poetics cannot insist on the primacy of one language, or on rules for using a language. As a poetics of relation, it will be "latent, open, multilingual in intention, directly in contact with everything possible."[36] In other words, rather than clinging to resemblances between different things, differences will be cherished for their capacity to produce something else. A trans-Pacific poetics bears primarily on what may or may not come to pass, rather than on what a general consensus deems already is. The goal for such a poetics, as for any kind of thought-in-becoming, is not to develop a general idea or model that would stand out from, or transcend, the world from which it comes. Instead, the goal is to create something new at ground level.[37] Generalities don't abolish differences; rather, becomings *free* differences from prior determinations of what is true or acceptable.

----

36 Édouard Glissant, *Poetics of Relation*, trans. Betsy Wing, 2006 ed. (Ann Arbor: University of Michigan Press, 1997), 32.

37 Paraphrasing Massumi, *A User's Guide to Capitalism and Schizophrenia*, 98.

RÍOS DE CISNES

PAULO HUIRIMILLA

I.

El río de cisnes que baja su espuma
Al mar de la página blanca
Hurga la roja cresta y el cuello negro
En los signos de la lamilla.
Gaviotas vocean en el arrebol del otoño
Que ha deshojado los árboles.
El río de cisnes ha disminuido su caudal
Su plumaje se lo ha llevado la negra marea.

II.

Los ensangrentados cisnes del río
Ya no pueden vender sus verduras
Pues las aguas con que riegan
Están forradas con metal.
Aterrizan aquellas aves en el patio
De un niño cisne poeta quien lo envuelve
Con su blanca mirada.

III.

Mi hijo Ave Veloz que amanece dibuja
Cuatro aves de negro cuello
Una es su madre quien lo lleva arriba de su espalda
Otro soy yo mismo quien sigue y dirige el agua
El viento y las nubes del paisaje:
Un ave de estas somos ensimismados
por el sol en el dibujo.

IV.

El signo del cisne del que habla Martínez
Aparece y no como significante
Troquelado también es el hombre entonces
Que ve en la orilla del camino
Cuatro criaturas volando
Debajo del mismo lenguaje.

V.

El lago formado por la sangre de Licarayén
Hundida el agua y la tierra
Expoliadas
A cuyas aves canta Lucila
En el idioma de los Licanantay y del mundo
Porque sólo quedan ellos
Otros
Han sido desplazados por ley y carabina
A la cordillera pelada para que olvidemos
Lo nuestro.

VI.

Mallarmé tu proyecto poético absoluto
Pudo tal vez ser
Escribir sobre miles de cisnes en invierno
Con múltiples palabras en una sola página
O decir de memoria poemas
Que representen los signos de la imaginación
Como Rubén Darío o Alfonsina Storni
Cuyo sueño frente al mar se respira en silencio.

VII.

Oye Lucila Fantasma ya he subido
Al huemul al hombro
Y al otro lado a un Pingangu
Color albino
Mutro le decimos
Hijo de un ave encanto
Que ha salido al borde del lago
Amar a la gansería
Que no vuela en los humedales
Ahora cubierto de pesado metal.

VIII.

Doy vueltas en el desierto de la isla como el cisne negro de cresta roja.
Alrededor vuelo buscando la laguna imaginada.
He visto en esto otros cisnes negros de cresta roja.
Ver también el mundo con sus cuatro direcciones.
A una la veo danzar y cantar como lo hacía su abuela
y las abuelas de sus abuelas

y pintar una tela blanca con muchos puntos de colores
que son los sueños paralelos de mis abuelos desaparecidos
quien hablan por mi saliva.
Han robado a los hijos de los cisnes negros de cresta roja
Lo han hecho volar a las ciudades y cuidar su ganado
Aves hermanas quienes no han vuelto.
Que naden ahora los cisnes Koori con todas sus serpientes del arco iris
Que las han creado
Que busquen por debajo del agua el alga
Que las hará respirar eternamente contra el olvido.
El cisne negro de cresta roja se me aparece en otra isla
en una página
Pero su color es más luminoso que la rebeldía.

IX.

Lenon veo dos cisnes completamente blancos en el
Támesis
Yo les canto mientras se levanta la
lluvia
y la policía recoge los
cuerpos
De los enajenados de este mundo quienes
ven aquellos signos que nadan por el paisaje de
esta lúgubre ciudad vigilada.

X.

De dos andan en el mar los negros cuellos
Y los cuerpos nadan por entre los sargazos y la página negra
La lluvia ácida moja su plumaje y ellos se picotean
buscando parte del arco iris en el agua
suben a orillar el río y se bañan después de la lluvia
esta nuestra ave que un poeta ha dicho cortarle el cuello
y un músico la ha hecho danzar en el lago
yo mismo las llamo desde la playa de los petrificados alerces
y ellas nos siguen y emprenden vuelo
por el aire cubierto de humo y ceniza.

RIVERS OF SWANS[38]

I.

The river of swans sprays foam
On the ocean of the white page,
Searching for the red crest and black neck
In the signs of the lamilla.
Seagulls shout out in the red glow of autumn
Leaves stripped from the trees.
The river of swans has diminished
Its plumage taken by the black tide.

II.

The bloodstained swans of the river
Can sell their vegetables no longer:
The waters that irrigate
Are full of metals.
The birds land in the courtyard
Of a young swan, a poet who envelopes the patio
With his white gaze.

III.

My son, Ave Veloz, awakes to draw
Four birds with black necks
One is his mother who takes him up on her back
Another is of me, who follows and channels the water
The wind and clouds of the landscape:
We are absorbed
By the sun of the picture.

IV.

The sign of the swan of which Martínez talks
Appears but without meaning
So the man is also die-cast
Who sees from the shore

---

38 English version first published in Stuart Cooke, "Two Mapuche Poets: Leonel Lienlaf and
   Paulo Huirimilla (introduction and translations)," in *HEAT 22: The Persistent Rabbit*, ed.
   Ivor Indyk (Atarmon: Giramondo, 2010), 58–62.

Four creatures flying
Beneath the same language.

V.
The lake filled by the blood of Licarayén
The sunken water and earth
Exploited
Birds to whom Lucila sings
In the language of the Licanantay and the world
Because only they remain
Others
Have been displaced by law and rifle
To the mountains stripped so that we might forget
What is ours.

VI.
Mallarmé your entire poetic project
Could have been, perhaps,
To write about thousands of swans in winter
With multiple words on only one page
Or to speak from memory poems
Representing the signs of the imagination
Like Rubén Darío or Alfonsina Storni
Whose dream before an ocean breathes in silence.

VII.
Listen Lucila Fantasma I've already lifted
The serf onto my shoulder
And onto the other one a *Pingangu*
Colour albino
Mutro we say
Son of an enchanted bird
Who has left the bank of the lake
For folly
Who doesn't fly in the wetlands
Now covered with heavy metals.

VIII.
I turn around in the island desert like the black swan with red crest.
I fly around looking for the inland sea.
I have seen it in these other black swans with red crests.

To also see the world with its four directions.
I see one dance and sing the way her grandmother did
and the grandmothers of her grandmothers
and she paints a white fabric with many spots of colour
which become the parallel dreams of my kidnapped grandparents
who speak through my saliva.
They have stolen the children of the black swans with red crests
They have been made to fly to the cities and care for their cattle
Bird sisters who have not returned.
May you swim now, Koori swans with all your rainbow snakes
That you've created
May you search beneath the water for the seaweed
That will make your snakes breathe eternally against oblivion.
The black swan of red crest appears to me on another island
On a page
But its colour is more luminous than rebellion.

IX.

Lennon sees two completely white swans in the
Thames
I sing to them while the rain
thickens
and the police collect the
bodies
Of the world's alienated, who
see those signs swimming across the landscape
of this gloomy guarded city.

X.

In pairs the black necks walk on the ocean
And the bodies swim between the black page and the sargassos
The acid rain wets their feathers and they peck at themselves
searching for part of the rainbow in the water
they climb to the river's edge to bathe after the rain
these our birds whose necks should be cut says a poet
a musician made them dance on the lake
myself I call them from the beach of the petrified cypress
and they follow us and launch into flight
through the air choked with fumes and ash.

Rubén Darío—(1867–1916), born in Nicaragua, the most important modernist in Hispanic literature.

la lamilla—a coffee-coloured seaweed eaten by the swans.

Licarayén—a young virgin sacrificed in order to calm the fury of Añuñauca Volcano, which today is known more commonly as Osorno Volcano.

Licanantay—indigenous people from the north of Chile.

Lucila—Lucila Godoy Alcayaga, Gabriela Mistral's real name.

Juan Luis Martínez—Chilean poet, says that in a poem it is only signification which is important.

Mutro—(Mapuzugun) an albino swan, which is generally of a golden colour.

petrified cypress—the *alerce* is known as the Patagonian cypress, common in Southern Chile.

Pingangu—(Mapuzugun) a swan.

Alfonsina Storni—(1892–1938) a major Argentinean poet of the postmodernist movement.

Ave Veloz—"Fast Bird," another name for Lautaro.

BIBLIOGRAPHY

Bernstein, Charles. "Poetics of the Americas." *Modernism/Modernity* 3, no. 3 (1996): 1–23.

Chihuailaf, Elicura. *Recado Confidencial a Los Chilenos*. Santiago: LOM, 1999.

Cooke, Stuart. "Two Mapuche Poets: Leonel Lienlaf and Paulo Huirimilla (Introduction and Translations)." In *Heat 22: The Persistent Rabbit*, edited by Ivor Indyk, 45–62. Atarmon: Giramondo, 2010.

de Landa, Manuel. *A Thousand Years of Nonlinear History*. 2003 ed. New York: Zone Books, 1997.

Deleuze, Gilles, and Félix Guattari. *A Thousand Plateaus: Capitalism and Schizophrenia*. Translated by Brian Massumi. London & New York: Continuum, 2004.

Dyson, Freeman. "Our Biotech Future." http://www.nybooks.com/articles/20370.

Fogarty, Lionel. "For I Come—Death in Custody." In *Macquarie Pen Anthology of Aboriginal Literature*, edited by Anita Heiss and Peter Minter, 92. Sydney: Allen & Unwin, 2008.

--. *Minyung Woolah Binnung (What Saying Says): Poems and Drawings*. Southport: Keeaira Press, 2004.

--., and Philip Mead. "Lionel Fogarty in Conversation with Philip Mead." http://jacketmagazine.com/01/fogartyiv.html.

--., Yvette Walker, and Kargun Fogarty. *Yerrabilela Jimbelung: Poems About Friends and Family*. Southport: Keeaira Press, 2008.

García, Mabel, Hugo Carrasco, and Verónica Contreras. *Crítica Situada: El Estado Actual Del Arte Y La Poesía Mapuche*. Temuco: Universidad de la Frontera, 2005.

Glissant, Édouard. *Poetics of Relation*. Translated by Betsy Wing, 2006 ed. Ann Arbor: University of Michigan Press, 1997.

Massumi, Brian. "Like a Thought." In *A Shock to Thought: Expression after Deleuze and Guattari*, edited by Brian Massumi, xiii-xxxix. London & New York: Routledge, 2002.

--. *A User's Guide to Capitalism and Schizophrenia: Deviations from Deleuze and Guattari*. 1996 ed. Cambridge, Mass.: MIT Press, 1992.

McCarthy, Bridie. "At the Limits: Postcolonial and Hyperreal Translations of Australian Poetry." PhD Thesis, Deakin University, 2006.

Mead, Philip. *Networked Language: Culture & History in Australian Poetry*. North Melbourne: Australian Scholarly Publishing, 2008.

Rajchman, John. *The Deleuze Connections*. Cambridge & London: MIT Press, 2000.

Rojas, Gonzalo, and Peter Minter, eds. *Espejo De Tierra (Earth Mirror)*. Canberra: Chilean Embassy, 2008.

Woese, Carl R. "A New Biology for a New Century." *Microbiology and Molecular Biology Reviews* 68, no. 2 (2004): 173–86.

BREAKING UP WITH H.D.

SEAN LABRADOR Y MANZANO

[What eviscerates you?]

1.

Ill + Kano = Sick American

I am the pun made possible
I am a Sick American made possible
an Illokano made possible
according to craniometrists,
I am possible from a long line of head-hunters
dermatologists insist lexical diffusion, are we how
from the waste down
from the waist down
you cannot see their collapsibility and error
their unmeasured navels

Coraopolis do well in poor soil. Lobelia too. Unmistakably my lover's hair, a woman of time-release capsules, of explosives and lightning, the week's missal: the unnatural pinoy puns. Correction: I am not pun/ning. Come eat I promise not to share thorns look for me

in the *Doctrina Christiana* there is no room for busos. Bamboo baskets straddle Santo Tomas river bank. Chicken entrails talonka. Here they tried his lunacy. I am now this small I walk into the green room and Christ was a madman serving livers of himself

so I set the house on fire because neurological damage can take strange forms. Maple waffles the ermine in sleep. I have seen wrinkled penises at nudist camps beyond the Farallones drug lords horde pelicans. Fluorescent embryos want nocturnal manicures.

Kielbasa is not everyone's red herring I am blind and you stand behind me when a good looking gal is obscene with jack cheese, but that ain't no tumor in the casserole, what did you gain by taking on the ex-wife, Sisyphus loads his cart with golden squash, and trades

bugle corn when Orpheus is no afterlife penned beyond. Have you at six years old caterwauled gelatinous payload and smiled for scorching Asia? The fontanel strange. The navel stranger beneath oilskin subduct palay moonless stirrups measure syncope

Where do we meet if not Intramuros?

[What eviscerates you?]

and there she traces
dragons opposing themselves
born to his third eye
Indra effaced from lotus

bronchioles ill luminate and ill embrace, insurgent clavicle in dark spaces in dark
faultlines in dark eccentricities in dark corridors tulips silent I-5 soft shoulder
north bound abrade walled cities commuted sentence discords syntax unmetered
synthesis in

dark orbits synchronous captive in native light malingering emplotments confess
charade. Dark invaginate shoals sustain infection in contrite margin. O fugitive
time. O fugitives. Deceptions selected publicly. Slip and now there is one. Our hands
cannot covertly hold:

The grace wafted remembers her birth control.
The grace stayed in her futon most days bled.
The grace hidden wouldn't keep it anyways.

Is there an honest woman among them?
Is there an honest woman?
Whom hope defines?

We at least promised nothing

Dark calyxes.
Dark determinates
Dark androeciums
Dark Continents

In mirror appear closer than objects
robust debris in the timeless infinitive
Venus infers white war, the daughter not born

But she wouldn't keep her anyways.

Where do we meet if not Intramuros?

[What eviscerates you?]

He will pay the bar fine. In his hotel room, they will strip down.
She will finger his waves. His ribs cage disaster.

He will shower and dry himself. The fogged mirror acknowledges
the Republic of the Philippines for extending assistance in
the making of a whore. No Pilipina was harmed

in Apocalypse Now
in The Year of Living Dangerously
in An Officer and a Gentleman
in Missing in Action
in Hamburger Hill
in Platoon
in Born on the Fourth of July

and in this film.
what fortress is your color?
how much candlepower requires your suicide?

she left a shadow in my bed.
he continues to sleep in it.
One of these days he will stop believing.

somewhere in this room not this room
cities spur gold tunics
beleaguered minarets winter slumberless

some inactity or inanity or inactivity
needful fucking, they are psychopomps
circumventing transept and reinventing cervix

for every ligation there is job security
negritos paddle off ramps, dust boys and dust girls jig hours
for babe's chaste hypoxia disarm dowager

[No. She will never meet the whore I am thinking about.]

Where do we meet if not Intramuros?

SEAN LABRADOR Y MANZANO · 157

[What eviscerates you?]

4.

for every woman there is an addict
bundoks transcribe mother's scop,
for son's enlightened hubris, stations of the cross

in the rain not horrified, children sell sampaguita
tamaraw collects bar fine good money
psychopomps enraftered, chariot leaves

swank suits speak in dollars cut lines
g.r.o.s are gigolo's comfort, two steps
wedded stigma, cave's clerestory

I'm tracing the bowsprit, hand of diminished life
lines, jaundiced vesicles of a murdered ilustrado,
simultaneously uvula and pudendum, mind parting

a balaisong, going where I must go, and you
a Dark Continent Companion, recipient of all things
written and dreamt from that sleepy place at the edge of the sea.

New Terneuzen, the dream that once was Dutch Ilocandia

Where do we meet if not Intramuros?

[What eviscerates you?]

5

Claimants seize gulag archipelago's faith in metaphor. What compels them to leave Intramuros and follow me to where horizons collide? Hammers hand them out. Serendipity turns each. Compel a nail as nails compel them are compelling as nails.

Everyspace for a nail. Everyspace between another nail. Measure nails for spaces measured. Do we ask how busos demand the placement of nails? Ragdolls comply and offer hands! Correct the color of my lens, resist a fetid tongue. Slough spines of missals.

Slough polyps of new desert. Masonry optic tongues febrile. Abrupt pudendum rocks baby's first shoes through rattle snake grass. Slough plates of dying redwood and dying oak tumble down dandelion parachute snow, the debris bed tumble down. Should I

continue to adore the one who has left me Cordilleras the one who has left me the receding berm. Appalachians reef Magellan's ghost fleet divorced of fiction and war tumble down shocktroops tumble down sappers tumble down rumors of war

only a six year old tumbles down in his head broods Peacemakers and Minutemen there is a woman who needs to listen to a man before his darker fictions of Peacemakers Minutemen Tridents Tomahawks Sidewinders Hellfires. There is a woman who needs

to listen to klaxons and fusillades there is a woman that this man does not need goosesteps and tanks there is this woman that this man does not need
in Beirut's firing line in Bataan's march in Binalonan's last stand

the tanks roll and there is this man a paddy shark eludes.

Explain endorphin to her and you're a better man.
Explain the sacred collapses, and she finds the familiar in you also collapses.
Explain barbed wire

and bittermelon trellising barbed wire and the many habits raking arms across barbed wire for fruit

and perhaps she will marry you.

She will marry you despite calumny and calamity.
She will bury her sins and marry you because you are still novel.

But if you don't explain it to her, then so much the better unmarried.

Where do we meet if not Intramuros?

[What eviscerates you?]

6.

Drive into the desert, a *black rider* crossing the bridge and pacify the *howling wilderness*.

Katonk

Do you hear the hammering?

Katonk

The anvil of our nakedness.

Katonk

A galleon?

Katonk

The novelty of its cannonade.

Katonk

To be lifted lifted in to place.

Arclight

She was never six years old with the congenital slant.

It is a diverse delta.

Where do we meet if not Intramuros?

Regimes change when monopolies cannot accessorize. When contents of Balikbayan boxes are known. How nation functions when in compliance, it cannot. I had buried myself into her. And because I buried myself into her was I not promoted to her bed.

I was going on a trip and found her in that bed, curled and mercurial. I was going on a trip and was bound to a bed. The devalue of my modernism, iliacs crest. Beneath the arena, Luna spoils retiarius, his passion appeals conviction. Her punitive kiss.

Where do we meet if not Intramuros?

[What eviscerates you?]

Does Valium taste like...? Rebar in thalamus. Throb of concrete and chainlink fence? Listen, a dharma needs his loneliness and he is there, the son needs his torch bearers and he is there, the androgene needs his sex and he is there, the misanthrope needs his society

and he is there, and the pallbearers what do they need that brings them here? a body. And he is there, half-naked blonde blemish a register of faith? He takes the form of a word burnt upon two lips. Nuestra eden perdido. And now what will I say when I emerge?

Where do we meet if not Intramuros?

[What eviscerates you?]

Castillejos?

Ask any Asuang for directions.
Ask any Museum Guard for the Asuang.
Ask any Museum Guard if she is Asuang.
Ask any Department of Tourism for directions to the nearest Museum.

But when the concierge monsters the transgenital matrix, I cannot claim its antecedent.
The inadmissible hyphen reports fidelity's hatchet job. She's obviously untrammeled,
an apprentice bellsheep with sheared bangs, strums gentle pleats, a hollow reminder.

I will tell you the name of our child,
I can hurt you the only way I know how.

Where do we meet if not Intramuros?

9.

Dissidents are despondent when censors ignore correspondence. Take the roach out of your mouth when I am talking to you. When Theodore Roosevelt ordered Subic Naval Base built, did he imagine durable goods attracting duwendes when fishing on Good

Friday was taboo. Billboards advertise Spring fashion. Now, how can flagellists ignore mestizas thinly railed? Soft drinks supplant suka. Please explain the lexical fitness of the imperial grammar. It is no secret I enjoyed the aspirated butterfly's nimble flight

> feckless
> serene
> finite
> wonder
> wonder
> her
> nascent
> ascent
> killing
> jar
> palm
> oil
> waxing
> naphthalene

are they not lugubrious the Bond girls competence trusses lumbar. Mycorrhizal wonderings are not speculative. Stab bindings return rites of return the vulgar mass listen listen the vulgar tongues securing ghosts while socialists and communists gather the Fab

Mab. When served chocolate meat, did the Avengers recoil? Dust children because napalm sticks. What will I remember: surface effects inadvertent and "inequivalent mirroring" or the inadvertent and "inequivalent mirroring" surface effects.

Where do we meet if not Intramuros?

[What eviscerates you?]

10.

Talinghagas are known to reveal themselves as themselves. Keep your head out of the water. Unmarked, Indra now refuses to surface from his dream. Captive audience is panoptic's sense of humor, the gulag archipelago is encouraged in so much a kuliglig

needs an imagist, an imagist needs a kuliglig. When plans a to y fail, z explodes the intersection. The family business is stimulus package. There's nothing wrong with narcotics when you don't use them yourself because writing will get you killed.

The zoning board will see to it. A labandera washes three loads before breakfast. Humanity is when I hide my socks from her. Her hands are hung to dry when sestinas move the movement. Are your fingers blue? What happens when anarchists fuck

pleasure models? Are we not annulled when HD sleeps? Endymion awake in the bedlam of your pasture. Shall son repeat in father's shadow? Shall father repeat in his father's absence? Day Parent is not Dead Beat when economy slouches, when son pronounces

consonants absent in gulag speech:

> Distruc-t
> Construc-t
> Instruc-t
> Induc-t
> Conflic-t
> Instinc-t
> Inflec-t
> Inflic-t
> Infec-t
> Reac-t
> Ac-t
> Rejec-t
> Subjec-t
> Objec-t
> Sculp-t
>
> Woof
> Woof
> Woof

Where do we meet if not Intramuros?

[What eviscerates you?]

11.

The facts are, says Adolescent Bacchus. The wrinkled doorframe. The carotic
notes back labor. Contractions typeset plaintive amniocentesis, like Madonna's
ovate child, mannered and baroque, an inchoate nimbus, dust children cloy

impetuousness, to be Caravaggio's avocation, brush meconium, the fontanel's
trillium, chiaroscuro: lumbago's idiom. How much to report war. Revel in
the occupied language the empire will teach me in its institute. Hear snipes!

A badge remedies. Projec-t his and his face. Projec-t what keeps me from sleep.
A badge remedies. To murder his and his face. To murder what keeps me from sleep.
A badge remedies. Such is my attenuated counsel. O chambered bright breech metal.

How I am not in compliance when the imperial grammar judges, elusive T.

What brings me here? The Dutchman on the horizon? I am a minor incident.
Consequence of a failed grammar. HD does not understand T-lessness is resistance.
How will I circulate when the ragdoll whispers derivatives? Cut flow artery. Trace

white pickets. Honor the addictive personality. Measure circumference. Measure
permission between hamate and capitate. Measure everything no longer between us.
This is how I will tremble when somaticists decide the distributive theory of limbs.

Je me ces vers!
Je me ces vers!
Je me ces vers!

Tamaraw steers lazy labrador's plot and plodding.

My muddled graft:

FFFFF   FFFFF

PAAAA   PAAAA

Puck   Puck

Fuck   Fuck

Where do we meet if not Intramuros?

12.

A vacant room for courting, dark discrete antimonianisms, to be seen published, perhaps in more than one poem. How timeless to stare at cunt waiting for prophecy. How to hurt her. What do I know about fucking? That it is the woman who talks in the middle

of fucking. All who will ignore will ignore them and their foray in to the night. They will ignore their stoicism for indifference. They will never speak their names. It is the only violence left. They will stare out that open window and greet St. Ignatius. They will

not allow for fascination or stillness of their blighted kiss and awake unrequited parchment. How we signed the deed. Dark Cypriots track abject arms in the lunette of a crude prairie. Strawberry Creek's cholera should revoke license. Gladly we did

not vow beneath the elder Buckthorn. The Dryad demands justice and I had courted its jurisdiction but how the jury favors promiscuity. I take my place among the beloveds. Sulfites are mangoes luster. Sweetness perjures. Yes, what brings me here to serve had

HD read Machado's "El Loco," had "El Loco" inspired Chagall's "White Crucifixion," had the "White Crucifixion's" flag-foreshadow gulag archipelago's premature independence then this is how I will shatter. This is how arms shatter. Heurtebise wake

up! Bring me my nails. And wake up that Longinus too. Bring me his spear. HD's imperial grammar wounds, surcease and seamless when her mouth supports the advertising of bombs, legs are stroboscopic when netted. Slumber slumber and retire

from the Convention of the Sea. But when Damay means compassion can one lose articulation when nailed to the cross? How shall my opioids come packaged? A vision thing. Recovered from her appetite, Rose Window's twenty five Buspar pills fit palm.

Where do we meet if not Intramuros?

How does one choose not to return, the way I return. I am returning.

> Agsubliac Pay!
> Agsubliac Pay!
> Agsubliac Pay!

In to the future, and refuse her grammar. What quimera am I? A MacArthur's Son, an Illokano, pun made possible by the Treaty of Paris, a lepidopterist, a war correspondent, a Sunshine Boy, an Irish Tenor, a salvaje, a pintado, a feroce. I am all of them and none.

A Day Parent. A Ghostly Father. Longinus overdetermine your spear. I offer you an Asuang to cut and flow. Cross the hermeneutic posture. HD's fraud vows eviscerate. Pallbearers! Pallbearers! Raise sail and remember when our town was Restless. When I

was first haunted I was profligate. Here are pericardia boxed between soul wounds. Crocodiles in the cress spared me a life. Two soul wounds for the price of one nail. But these feet cannot decide being lifted lifted in to place. How else can I conceive?

Will damo thin blood? Can betel nut exhaust diaphragm? Can we now examine the fitness of marriage between war correspondent and war correspondent's bride? Median vein are these connections sever intermodal commerce between maritime rivals.

> hindsight
> bundok
> debt
> envenerate
> spite
> fob

Loewinsohn, have you ever met such a malevolent spirit? Raised the apple high against you? Tested the flexibility of your tongue? That you ran from the City? How shall I imagine her now? Liebestod's solace is clapboard contract's endocrine disruptor is the time release for everyone sitting in darkness there is a beveled fritillary concupiscence translates. Yes. She did not hear me. My lisping. My slippage. My T-lessness. My senescence. My consonance. My dissonance. My correspondence.

My gibberish. But alas, poor Gibor. The metatext message. My palimpsest. My conscription. Pressed to serve her appetite. Speaking can get you killed. Dubious lovers will see to it. Yes, let us be logical and not pledge. Her hands query. How ashamed of

Where do we meet if not Intramuros?

14.

My stigma? My sepsis? My speech acts? My mummer's pride? My archipelago tongue? No! My gulag tongue emerged when taught properly. My twinned tsismis thwarting Thomasites plundered because Tagalog is this much pig iron and this much phosphorous

because jeepney feelings genetic inferiority she doesn't know learned behavior because barkada are peers take off your cues not of any conscious action because balut are eggs of cosmic distress in some kind of acid wash because landong's hypnotic shadows all

the time in the van conversion's rearview mirror and it is hard to explain because orasyones are weird prayers if you noticed because usbong's aural potty trained when going number 2 because indios in the seminary of the insane because brown is the color

that dreams Barrows, because the cherub casts coins are lovely and diving for them is figment of malnutrition because most loyal of colonial subjects, viscera suckers guard Chagall's cats. Garrote petal petulance is reenactment effigy on the way to the wedding

carpet threadbare, white gold administers false diamond, these lips elide surface effects barreling of whiteness fouls compass, what brings me here to be owed and owned.

St. Vincent, the scourge, marks the womb kicks plentiful, untie the umbilical frown.

Tumble down.

Tumble down.

I shall speak correckly now.

I shall speak correckly now.

I shall speak correckly now.

Titulus reads: Poet.

So let us examine how we do not fit in each other's lives anymore.

FROM *POETA EN SAN FRANCISCO*

BARBARA JANE REYES

1. NOT PREVIOUSLY ENCOUNTERED

silken forms from far east slice china melons.
silent sylphs, sampaguita and seaspray aromas
wafting. of jade gardens, terraced mountainsides,
bamboo thickets, some primordial magic,
some concealed eden awaits his cartography.

[o sodo i biti bo we wo no dato to o koti
wa powi ha ko itu boso
wo kadiu te ginida
hosi he hosi ibi a tidi ti we so
we ha no di te bati a mu
be hibi hi hosi a tidi
te ginida a o te te sodi a be te
te hosi a we ta te ginida ha ibudi adu a kuwibi onamiti we pi si
te inimi i se we mo be kadipu
we we si o ti wilo we dupi we si
we ko ba i te so
we go soli we a hugi a tisi
o mi i po o sodo wo wi ku o o gi]

2. NEVER USED BEFORE NOW

the scribe expresses profound disillusion—
the edifices of his own empire are lackluster.
he tastes others' tongues and tang so curious,
so fresh, he discovers they are to his liking.
he names himself sage eradicator of ennui.

ꪔ 3
ꪔ ꪔ ꪔ ꪔ ꪔ ꪔ ꪔ ‖ ꪔ ꪔ ꪔ ꪔ ꪔ ꪔ ꪔ ꪔ ꪔ ꪔ ꪔ
ꪔ ꪔ ꪔ ꪔ ꪔ ꪔ ꪔ ꪔ ꪔ ꪔ ꪔ ꪔ ꪔ ꪔ ꪔ ꪔ ꪔ ꪔ ꪔ ꪔ
ꪔ ꪔ ꪔ 3 ꪔ ꪔ 3 3 ꪔ ꪔ ꪔ 3 ꪔ ꪔ ꪔ 3 ꪔ ꪔ
ꪔ ꪔ ꪔ ꪔ 3 3 ꪔ ꪔ ꪔ ꪔ ꪔ ꪔ ‖ ꪔ ꪔ ꪔ ꪔ ꪔ 3 ꪔ ꪔ ꪔ
ꪔ ꪔ ꪔ ꪔ ꪔ ꪔ ꪔ ꪔ ꪔ 3 ꪔ ꪔ ꪔ ꪔ ꪔ ꪔ ꪔ ꪔ
ꪔ ꪔ ꪔ ꪔ

ꪔ 3
ꪔ ꪔ ꪔ ꪔ ꪔ ꪔ ꪔ ‖ ꪔ ꪔ ꪔ ꪔ ꪔ ꪔ ꪔ ꪔ ꪔ ꪔ ꪔ
ꪔ ꪔ ꪔ ꪔ ꪔ ꪔ ꪔ ꪔ ꪔ ꪔ ꪔ ꪔ ꪔ ꪔ ꪔ ꪔ ꪔ ꪔ ꪔ ꪔ
ꪔ ꪔ ꪔ 3 ꪔ ꪔ 3 3 ꪔ ꪔ ꪔ 3 ꪔ ꪔ ꪔ 3 ꪔ ꪔ
ꪔ ꪔ ꪔ ꪔ 3 3 ꪔ ꪔ ꪔ ꪔ ꪔ ꪔ ‖ ꪔ ꪔ ꪔ ꪔ ꪔ 3 ꪔ ꪔ ꪔ
ꪔ ꪔ ꪔ ꪔ ꪔ ꪔ ꪔ ꪔ ꪔ 3 ꪔ ꪔ ꪔ ꪔ ꪔ ꪔ ꪔ ꪔ
ꪔ ꪔ ꪔ ꪔ

[we yilo go a we diyiwi we pa po so a lati a we we du po mo o mo pogiti te ki a pisi

itilidiyi mi ka diti i po ti si a po ti wi bodi a we te a we yu ipisali te wa noti a ko
popo a te ma noti o si kosi o o mota kosi i uli te ko be o ta pilosi a we a so o o he a
mi a wiu digi

a te i wa si o tu so wa soti i ladi go a yu to ti no o dako hoko te we ha noti bu tu a
mimodi i komu]

3. JUST ARRIVED

a fool, he believes his boots to be the first
markers of civilization. women, bare-breasted,
offer fragrant garlands. lovely, their smiles,
their thick rivers of henna ebony hair.
pintada, he calls them for their tinted skins.

ᜃ ᜃ ᜂ ᜊᜓᜎᜐᜆᜃ ᜎ ᜇ ᜃ ᜐᜃ ᜂ ᜂ ᜒ ᜃ ᜃᜓ ᜐᜃ ᜊᜓᜆᜓᜎ ᜃ
ᜃ ᜃ ᜃᜃᜊ ᜎ 3 ᜃ ᜃᜒ ᜃ ᜃᜃ ᜂᜃ ᜐᜃ ᜃ ᜂᜆ 3 ᜃ ᜃᜊ ᜂ
ᜎᜓ ᜃ ᜂ ᜃ ᜎᜓ ᜂᜆ ᜃ ᜐᜃ ᜃ ᜃᜊ ᜂᜆ ᜎ 3 ᜐᜊ ᜃ ᜎᜓ ‖ ᜃ
ᜂ ᜊᜓ ᜎᜒ ᜃ ᜎᜒ 3 ᜒ 3 ᜓ ᜃ ᜐ 3 ᜓ ᜎᜃ ᜃ ᜎ ᜓᜎᜒ ‖ ᜃ
ᜃ ᜓ ᜃᜊ ᜃ ᜃᜃ 3 ᜊᜓᜎ ᜃ ᜒ ᜒ ᜎᜓᜒ 3 ᜃ ᜎᜓᜂ ᜂ 3ᜒ

[a te we sipadatu ha ko to i wo we mi a tabo itu sidiyu to a ti titisi po o ti tuni a titi
wati ito a bali o ti tosa bi puwi ta wa ti pi bali a itu te tosa bali po o bosi a piwi

a we sibi hani a di o go o ka te i ka poma a he kopani

a te ka a asu te tuma o siyu to mi mi payi o a diyiwi mo oga]

4. CHANGED FOR THE BETTER

for every daemonic place he erects stone

archangels and infernos, exacts penance

from those driven underground, spills his seed,

his battle cry, his body presses firm dispensation.

he invents himself by extracting others' titles.

𖼖 𖼱 𖼛 𖼎 3 𖼊 𖼙 𖼗 𖼗 𖼊𖼗 𖼞𖼟 3 𖼗 𖼞𖼗 𖼗 𖼗 𖼟𖼗𖼗 𖼗𖼞
𖼊 𖼊𖼗 𖼖𖼞 𖼳 𖼞 𖼖 𖼞 𖼞𖼗 𖼊 𖼞 𖼱𖼗 𖼖 𖼗 𖼣3 3 𖼞 3𖼱 𖼖 𖼳
𖼊 𖼞𖼗 𖼞 𖼳𖼱𖼣 𖼱𖼞 𖼱 𖼱 3 𖼗 𖼊𖼗 𖼱𖼣 𖼞𖼗 𖼊 𖼞𖼗𖼣 𖼱𖼞
𖼖 𖼞𖼗 𖼊3 𖼗𖼳 𖼊 𖼗 𖼊𖼞 𖼱 𖼱𖼞 𖼞 𖼣 𖼖 𖼗 𖼊𖼱𖼞 𖼱 𖼱𖼗 𖼳
𖼖𖼞 𖼣3𖼣 𖼖 𖼗 𖼊𖼗 𖼖 𖼱𖼞 𖼱 𖼳 𖼞𖼱𖼗 𖼱 𖼞𖼞 𖼞𖼞 𖼱𖼗 𖼱
𖼖 𖼖 𖼱 𖼣3 𖼞 𖼱 𖼱𖼞 𖼱𖼱𖼞 𖼱𖼗 𖼖 𖼗 𖼱 𖼣𖼞𖼞 𖼎 𖼖 𖼞 3𖼗
𖼳𖼣 𖼞 𖼱𖼱𖼞 𖼎𖼳 𖼖 𖼗 𖼊 𖼞𖼗 𖼗 𖼣3 𖼖 𖼞𖼗𖼞𖼗 𖼞 𖼱𖼣 𖼞 3
3𖼞 𖼗 𖼞 ‖ 𖼖 𖼖 𖼗 𖼞 𖼞 𖼖 𖼞 ‖ 𖼖 𖼞 𖼚 𖼖𖼱 𖼗 𖼎 𖼞 𖼊

[a yu wo wa o wi mi to te witi kuni o te kati to te dinati tipi we wati abu i ki a bo
diya we bo puti a te sa o mo oga a du we dipi li dagosa gui ga gi o te wati pisu lati
we kutisa gui a komi wio hida we te wilu pa pali li so a te bimilo gi giti do abu sosi
a te wati a hadi pi di dipiti gi ibu ibu pati gi a a pi si i yu moli gapuli pati a te gi
singi ba a i oti dasi i tapai buka a te we liti te sa a itidoti i tusi i o odi te ko

a a te ko to a i

a i no aga to be me we]

5. RECENTLY OBTAINED OR ACQUIRED

wives from cherry blossoms catalogues and bars adjacent
to military bases. black market handguns, .45 caliber
samurais and angels. assault rifles nicknamed "shorty."
sexy clandestine WMDs. means of acquisition not in
question free enterprise as cyclical self-reinvention.

ᜃ ᜑ ᜇ ᜃ ᜊᜒ ᜆᜒ ᜊᜒ ᜎᜈ ᜑ ᜈᜓ
ᜈ ᜐ ᜎᜀ ᜃ ᜈ ᜁ ᜈᜒᜆ ᜈᜃ
ᜈ ᜆ ᜂ ᜃ ᜀᜀ ᜊᜒ ᜈᜓ ᜇᜊᜒ
ᜈ ᜃ ᜎᜀ ᜑ ᜊᜒ ᜈᜓ ᜃ ᜃ ᜀ ᜈ
ᜎ ᜃ ᜃ ᜃ ᜆᜀ ᜐ ᜃ ᜀᜆᜁ ᜃ ᜊᜒ
ᜃ ᜊᜒ ᜈᜓᜈ ᜃᜃ ᜆᜒ ᜃ ᜊᜓᜈᜒᜊᜒ

ᜎ ᜈᜓ ᜐ ᜊᜒ ᜑ ᜆ ᜈ
ᜐ ᜋᜀ ᜆ ᜀᜐ ᜀᜈ
ᜆᜃ ᜐ ᜑ ᜇ ᜐ ᜆᜒ ᜎ ᜃ ᜃ
ᜊᜒ ᜃ ᜎ ᜃᜊᜒ ᜃ ᜐ ᜋᜀ ᜆᜒ ᜀ

[we mi ha wa si ku sa ako mi puhi
pa i abo te po ga poli powi
yu ka bi o babo si payi hosi
yu wa abo mi si payi wi te bo po
a we we o libi i ti bilagi o koka
tu sa pipo wiu rili o sopisu

a poti i madi mi lo yu
i nibi la bii bapu
luwii mi hi i loku a te wa
kali to a tusa ti i nibi luki ba]

6. STRIKINGLY UNUSUAL

because she found nascence entering his field of view.
because his words lay waste to her disparaged homeland.
because he posited her simply as his other.
because he invoked her, a muse for signification.
because casualties of war are a necessary expenditure.

ᜥ ᜲᜦᜲ ᜐ ᜨᜲᜧ ᜨᜩᜲ
ᜐ ᜦᜲᜨᜲ ᜧᜲ ᜧ ᜦ ᜧ ᜧᜲᜈ ᜧ ᜤ
ᜤᜲᜧ ᜥ ᜤᜲᜧ ᜥ ᜤᜲᜧ
ᜧ ᜨ ᜐ ᜦ ᜦ ᜦ 3

ᜥ ᜨᜦ ᜤ ᜦᜲᜦ
ᜤ ᜧ ᜐᜦ ᜤ ᜦᜦᜲᜤ ᜧ ᜦ ᜦᜲᜧ 3 ᜨᜲᜧ ᜐᜲᜦ
ᜥ ᜤ ᜦ ᜧ ᜈ ᜤ ᜦ ᜧ
ᜦ ᜦᜲᜦ ᜧ ᜨᜲᜤ ᜦᜨ 3ᜧᜦ

[a piti i sopi soli
i desede mi do to be migi wi yu
pudibi a pudibi a pudibi
we so i ki ti lo o

a siti yu dipati
yu we ito pa kotoyi be dibi o sidi idi
a yu ha be go po pe mo
te moki ma sodopu nosi obihi]

7. LATEST IN SEQUENCE

please understand, if she does not tug at your heart strings,
then you will not see truths in her testimony. if you do not
believe your wars have ever assaulted her splintered form,
her fissured tribes, then you will not acknowledge her
as anything other than a cheaply constructed replica of you.

ᜌᜓ ᜇᜄᜒ ᜌᜓ ᜉᜒ ᜏᜒ ᜌᜓ ᜏᜒ ᜂ
ᜊᜒ ᜆᜒ ᜄ ᜈᜓ ᜆᜒ ᜋᜓ ᜁ ᜄᜓ ᜇᜒᜉᜒᜇᜒ ᜋᜓᜐ
ᜆᜓ ᜇᜒ ᜆᜓ ᜃᜒ ᜆᜒ ᜀᜏ
ᜆᜒ ᜎᜒᜊᜒ ᜉ ᜁᜎᜒ ᜁ ᜀᜆᜓ ᜁ ᜏᜒ
ᜆᜒ ᜉᜀᜇᜒ ᜊᜓᜆᜒᜉᜒ ᜀ ᜀᜇᜒᜇᜒ ᜌᜒᜎᜓ ᜏᜒ ᜀᜄᜓ
ᜂᜊᜒ ᜆᜒ ᜄ ᜁ ᜆᜒ ᜏᜒ ᜄᜇᜒ
ᜆᜒ ᜑᜓ ᜋᜒ ᜁ ᜄᜓ ᜂᜇᜒ
ᜁ ᜌᜓ ᜀ ᜃᜓᜋᜒ ᜇᜓ ᜆᜓ ᜆᜒ ᜈᜇᜓ ᜂ ᜆᜒ ᜇᜒᜊᜒ ᜃᜒᜀ
ᜉᜒᜐ ᜎᜒ ᜋᜒ ᜃᜓ ᜊᜒᜉᜓᜇᜒᜑ
ᜀ ᜁ ᜏᜒ ᜃᜓ ᜂ ᜆᜓ ᜋᜒ ᜌᜓ
ᜀ ᜉ ᜀ ᜃᜓᜉᜓᜐ

[yu dagi yu pi we yu we o
be ti ga no ti mo i go dipidi musi
to di to ki ti awa
te libi pa ili i atu i we
te paadi butipi a adidi yilu we agu
ubi te ga i te we gadi
te ho mi i go odi
i yu a komi do to te nado o te dibi kia
pisi li mi ko bipodiha
a i we ko o to mi yu
a pa a kopusa]

8. CURRENTLY FASHIONABLE

he speaks words that were never his to speak.
he speaks words that were never his to speak.
he speaks words that were never his to speak.
he speaks words that were never his to speak.
he does not know the gravity of such offense.

[i ma a pa we yu era pou
i ha ditete yu lo inu
i ko to yu a a go ki
wo ha ha a pi hidi pati
i a o inu no to ma pi
i wa yu ta bo ti ni wo
no i a ti po kabi
we ha o sa a o ro
li te be komi beti o]

pnlNi sig

pngini lm Ito dkil luso ariarih d n mN dyuh mddbo a mggh . a mN da a npopono n
mlulupi kiyno m mlki bri a Iv npktino biNi

pipi . wl pkig a kniy sig Nuni lgi allhI nmi . Ito luso n pngini a pklig s tun . p
lumuluh a lup dumdlis n apo a mN luh niy . p m byo sumisig a lup . a sbi niy tm n

Hidi alal s luwhti s diyo s dotin . a s simul a mgigi n nm . Ikinukuli n klNit a mN
Ol n abo pinpali n lup a ls

FROM *COMMONS*

MYUNG MI KIM

POLLEN FOSSIL RECORD

Book of Famine, Book of Attempt, Book of Money
Book of Labor, Book of Scribes
Book of Utterance, Book of Hollow Organs,
Book of Tending, Book of Wars, Book of Household,
Book of Protection, Book of Grief, Book as Inquiry

Swerves, oddities, facts, miscues, remnant—threnody and meditation—
the perpetually incomplete task of tracking what enters into the field of perception
(the writing act)—its variegated and grating musics, cadences, and temporalities

Book as specimen
Book as instruction

The book emerges through cycles of erosion and accretion

COMMONS elides multiple sites: reading and text making, discourses and disciplines,
documents and documenting. Fluctuating. Proceeding by fragment, by increment.
Through proposition, parataxis, contingency—approximating nerve, line, song

Velocity, the exultant and transitory glimpse of encounter

The inchoate and the concrete coincide

Desire for the encyclopedic // Interrogation of archive

Released into our moment, shaped as it is by geographical and cultural displacements,
an exponentially hybrid state of nations, cultures, and voicings

Even in the midst of (or perhaps especially in view of) a fully entrenched commodity
society, how might it be possible to render the infinitesimally divisible moment

The meaning of becoming a historical subject.

"APHORISMS ARE 'BROKEN KNOWLEDGE' THAT CREATE 'WONDER'," ADVANCEMENT, BACON

Because isolations occur

Uncover the ear

To give form to what is remote, castigated

The necessity of carving out [intuiting/enacting] one's own treatment of a particular arena of language

Social and psychic identifications that disrupt and (re)envision, to throw into question conventions of codifying

Form as interplay of mobile elements, actuated by the ensemble of movements developed within it

The comportment is one of experiment

The poem infiltrates, filters, avulses : nuance and gradation

"The fragment is that part of the totality of the work that opposes totality."
Aesthetic Theory, Adorno

The contrapuntal, the interruptive, the speculative

What is the work of household—the moral and just education of a child

The interrelation between populations and their environments

There is the discussion about shortages

A collapse in food production, socioeconomic differentiation, and poverty were the results

Social rules for distribution
Cultural rules for consumption

Feminization of poverty // Feminization of the problem of lived time
_____, a word that cannot be translated: it suggests, "what belongs to the people"

Modes, registers of   [collectivity

Human voice   range
                             (to) bursting
                             prayer

Sound's physicality [human longing

Of being in and affecting

Poets as "agents for the most arduous, most dangerous cause there is: to love the other, even before being loved." *Stigmata*, Cixous

To usher in   :   time action matter

"DATES TO IMPUGN AND DIVULGE"

The daily and the continuous.

"Lamenta" attempts to hold in relation these two indicatives, fixed time and cyclical time.

Chronicling lived time : registering the continuum of history.

Structurally, responding to the idea of the Metonic cycle, a cycle of nineteen years, transposed (mutated?) to the daily and the materiality of history.

Bound time (chronology) up against radicalized time (mutability of chronology).

To call into question, to disclose, to make common

THE IDEA OF ROMANIZATION

The ideas of translation, translatability, transliteration, transcription:

Bit, part, scattered phoneme, suggestion of sounds, a glitch of ear and tongue occurring in unrecognizable patterns: for a long time I dismissed (or couldn't fold in or hold) these random, skittish stutterings. However, once perceived as (made audible and tactile as) potential sounds in Korean or, for that matter, any number of languages (Middle English, Latin, French) that constitute "English," these roaming fragments fall into the writing. Yet, how to render their presence fully? Sometimes, this necessitated conjoining the English and Korean alphabets (ㅈ/jw) or (ee/어).

Rehearsals of conflating Korean and English texts, for example, in the body of a 14th century *sijo* or an alliterative English poem from about the same time. Set in concurrent motion, these texts were "translated" simultaneously. It is not the actual translation or even the state of translatability between the two texts that is intriguing but the possibilities for transcribing what occurs in the traversal between the two languages (and, by extension, between the two "nations," their mutually implicated histories of colonization, political conflicts, and so on). What is the recombinant energy created between languages (geopolitical economies, cultural representations, concepts of community)?

Rehearsals of listening: practicing sound and gesture between languages, between systems of writing. How physically (almost physiologically) impossible it is to pronounce or even imagine what Korean words are being depicted under the standard (standardized) romanization of Korean. The odd vowel blurs, the unclear consonant combinations. Poised between a spectral and real engagement with Korean. The practicing had to be one in which this specific formulation of ear, mouth, and tongue had to find a correspondence in "English"—oral, aural, and written. Practices in transliteration: comparing the standard romanization to what [I] might be said to be hearing: "sesang sarămdŭr-a" next to "sae sahng sah rham deul ah." Whose ears are at work? Where does the authority of romanizing reside? How might it be entered into otherwise?

A further rehearsal: being compelled to write down as exactly as possible the words of Olga Kim, speaking about her forty years of living in Siberia, and knowing fully that an atrophied, arrested, third grade Korean writing is what was available. What was missing? What was forgotten? What was never learned in the first place? What was and was not written "correctly"? Each of these instances is enunciative.

These rehearsals, not as description, but as activation—actively investigating how legibility is constructed and maintained, how "English" is made and disseminated.

What *is* English now, in the face of mass global migrations, ecological degradations, shifts and upheavals in identifications of gender and labor? How can the diction(s), register(s), inflection(s) as well as varying affective stances that have and will continue to filter into "English" be taken into account? What are the implications of writing at this moment, in precisely this "America"? How to practice and make plural the written and spoken—grammars, syntaxes, textures, intonations...

Counter the potential totalizing power of language that serves the prevailing systems and demands of coherence

Contemplate the generative power of the designation "illegible" coming to speech

Enter language as it factors in, layers in, and crosses fields of meaning, elaborating and extending the possibilities for sense making

Consider how the polyglot, porous, transcultural presence alerts and alters what is around it

DURATION

"This is to be sung"
"This is to be done"

The lyric undertakes the task of deciphering and embodying a "particularizable" prosody of one's living.

And in that process, inside the procedures of work and of work proceeding: node and pressure point, song making and song gesture. Track: descant, sedimentations, tributaries in any several directions. Show stress, show beat, show alterations in pitch and accentuals. Tempo ruptured, emended. A valence of first and further tongues. Elements of the lyric and its meditations The duration of the now, the now occurring, that manifests a time before.

A line's shape, vector, and motion interpolates perception and meter

A measure, a page, the book to embody the multivalent, the multidirectional—a cathexis of the living instant to the acuteness of history

Each sound trace, each demonstration of the line, each formal enunciation: aperture: conduit: coming into articulation, into the Imaginary—the lyric as it embodies the processural

The poem may be said to reside in disrupted, dilated, circulatory spaces, and it is the means by which one notates this provisional location that evokes and demonstrates agency—the ear by which the prosody by which to calibrate the liberative potential of writing, storehouse of the human

To probe the terms under which we denote, participate in, and speak of cultural and human practices—
To mobilize the notion of our responsibility to one another in social space

OUTRO: IF AND

SAWAKO NAKAYASU

If water is the new bridge

And if the new imperative no longer just to traverse some definable locale, but to live, swim, dive, puncture, excavate, recuperate, rearticulate some new, fluid passionate flight over and beyond the old boundaries, to carry forward past and ongoing histories of place, space, adamantly local geology and ecology, sometimes it is wet, no longer is it linear, singular, nor limited to a single geography, identity, notion of centrality,

If no longer *center,* but *adjacent,* if the center of the self is adjacent to the self according to old limitations of this or that culture, and the force of such jostling pressurizes the internal and external body, via Jai Arun Ravine,

If Stuart Cooke reminds us that Filipino literature is one of the world's major English-language literatures, and thus also that "The Centre Cannot Hold,"

If the adjacent, the border, the edges of the border, the wet edges of the porous tactile border—if these margins, and *The margin consumes the center and becomes the center* (DMC)[1],

If Lisa Samuels' wet contact, and then consciousness is electrifying,

If all of this is history, if all of this is capitalism (if most of the economy of Guam is U.S. military spending and the tourist industry),

If there are this many parallel English-language universes, *What is English now, in the face of mass global migrations, ecological degradations, shifts and upheavals in identifications of gender and labor?* (MMK),

Besides, why must we always be doing things in reaction to the term "American"? (ET),

---

1 Italicized phrases and lines are drawn from this book, followed by the initials of the writer in parentheses.

I dangle, therefore I am (SS),

If Pacific, if ring of fire, if earthquakes, if volcanoes. If the poet Craig Arnold, gone missing while hiking on a small Japanese volcanic island. If ring of fire vs. ring of war = violence of nature vs. violence of humans, if a volcanic mountain sprouts suddenly during war, *A cease-and-desist measure at the time of transcendental no-surrender* (CW),

If Monday in Samoa is Tuesday in most of the world is Wednesday in Kiritimati, aka Christmas Island—site of nuclear-weapons testing, also the largest coral atoll in the world,

To inhabit various sizes, scales, structures, land masses, movements, what is small, what is large, what is soil, is ground, is politics, what is a small press like Tinfish in a large body of water,

If resistance to colonialism, imperialism, resistance to the forgetting of such, resistance to silencing, to hegemony, assimilation, occupation,

If resistance and empathy
If resistance and continuum
If resistance and

> *magellan*
> *broughtcatholicsandwesternway*
> *newera*
> *japaneseforcesassumedcontrol*
> *u.s.troopsreclaimed* (LT),

If continuum: what is speakable, writable, audible, legible. What is legible vs. illegible in Lehua M. Taitano, what is the discomfort, where is the gap, what kinds of violence, what of the cultural and hegemonic violence of language,

If internet, and community, if Pinoy haiku, is Eileen Tabios *"talking back"* or "carrying colonialism," and so then what hay(na)ku. And if Melanie Rands makes space for engagement, activism, social progress,

If Jai Arun Ravine is guide, navigator, tourist, if belonging or not belonging, representing and not representing, if telling, retelling, knowing, knowing again, recuperating knowing, knowing differently, and if you are laughing, whether you laugh with, through, or at,

If avant-garde while also resisting the limits of a linear forwardness, and "Editing Tinfish and living in Hawai'i have also alerted me that the avant-garde cannot be defined so narrowly as it is by many scholars [...] But so few writers and editors open up the doors of the avant-garde to work that is not experimental in some few ways [...]. I would hope that Tinfish opens the field, perhaps even breaks it,"

If identity and that is not all
If identity and that is mixed race, mixed gender
If identity and mixed genre
If identity and *a queen of vehicular slumber,*
If *a dark-haired person,* if *a dark-eyed person,*
If *cis-gendered,* if *a fan of fluidity* (YWH),
If LGBTQIA+, if QTPOC,
If a single father,
If asked to *Sign on the straight line with whatever name is easiest to recall* (SS),

If transgender and transnational feminist concerns (JAR) can be bridged with so much ocean, *Where do we meet if not intramuros?* (SLM),

I want the sound of our voices to rise. Noise is unwanted sound sometimes based on trauma ... some military weapons can kill you before you can hear them (CSP),

If *Princess Abandoned's realm of death is not an oppressed space but a counter-patriarchal one where a woman can redefine herself. In this place,* a woman, the empty darkness, does not follow the logic of ownership (DMC),

If Albert Saijo, and the internment of Japanese Americans during WWII,

If war, if hard war, if history of war, and Don Mee Choi's *Hardly War,*

If "All cafés are wartime cafés during a time of war," and Sean Labrador y Manzano "can put push-ups in a resume. Push-ups lead to promotions. My son doing push-ups is empathy. He joins in once in a while. He thinks it is fun. Empathy is the opposite of war toy's appealing sympathetic magic,"

If *The map is not the territory* (MR),

> *please understand, if she does not tug at your heart strings,*
> *then you will not see truths in her testimony. if you do not*
> *believe your wars have ever assaulted her splintered form,*
> *her fissured tribes, then you will not acknowledge her*

as anything other than a cheaply constructed replica of you. (BJR),

To belong to a country that had instigated or continued or condoned or received or resisted violence, if this and every other kind of DMZ, the DMZ of Outer Space, to write from all the DMZs of the World, all the DMZs of the Word,

How many tunnels of aggression
How many tunnels of aggressive memory
Thick, aggressive memory

If in the lateral reach of an oceanic, a sensual moment of contact (ocean), and a verticality, controlled and uncontrolled airspace: *more specifically the space lying above a nation and coming under its jurisdiction*, and **READINESS**: *includes ability to deploy and employ without delays* (CSP),

If memory is demilitarized, and *Someone writes to me about the word "residue," how it lives in the DMZ between what is remembered and forgotten* (SS),

If inevitable forms of natural violence: the editing of this book began shortly after an earthquake in Christchurch, New Zealand (February 2011) and shortly before one in Tohoku, Japan (March 2011),

If the making of this book involved a moment of transit, moment of earthquakes, moment of being gratefully supported with funds from a university of a country who has been imperial, and colonial, and war, and war, and occupation,

If this book is underlined by its inescapable history, a history that threatens to be overwhelmed by a narrative of war,

And

To write from the micro and macro levels of time and geography. And ocean. And Oceania, *Te moana nui a Kiwa*—The great ocean of Kiwa (ME),

The 1985 Penguin Book of New Zealand Verse, the anthology Ian Wedde and Harvey McQueen edited which challenged the earlier 1960 Penguin Anthology of Allen Curnow's in its inclusion of Māori language waiata/poetry, giving the poetry of Aotearoa/New Zealand a heritage in two languages [...] New Zealand Poetry must always have been in two languages (at least), but this reality had been avoided up until the Wedde/McQueen anthology appeared (ME),

And so if poetry is knowledge-making, and knowledge-recuperating, and poetry is, in Barbara Jane Reyes, also myth-making, and the potential for poetry to connect the contemporary with a longer history, a wider context,

In the quest to diversify and grow more resilient, Huirimilla has decided that all language and meaning-making is of the earth. In doing so, he is not asking that language deny the local but, on the contrary, that we never forget its attachment to the local (SC),

And *distributed centrality* (LS)
And distributed English
And all the Englishes in this book, this world, that don't unite but persist anyway,
And internet linguistics, and the fluid wet digital electric English of TransEnglish,
Eileen Tabios says "I do know English,"

And this, too, can be anthology, and anthology can be porousness,
And I reject the inclusion-exclusion binary, and dip my arms into the water,
And the center of the book also spreads to the outside of this very hugging of the water,

Do I differentiate between the product of art the discussion of art the dissemination of art, or do I concern myself with the loaded boundaries between all of the above,

And these old wooden bridges can be salvaged by feeling and looking anew at these oceans, carrying us not forward but across the widening depths of memory and creation,

Imagining new formations of water and land and sky and all the language that lies in between them, gloriously threatening to make themselves known—

Melbourne & Tokyo
August–September 2016

BIBLIOGRAPHY

Choi, Don Mee. *Hardly War.* Seattle: Wave Books, 2016.

Cooke, Stuart. "The Centre Cannot Hold: Six Contemporary Filipino Poets." *Cordite Poetry Review,* November 1, 2012. Accessed September 20, 2016. http://cordite.org.au/chapbooks-features/the-centre-cannot-hold/.

Labrador y Manzano, Sean. "Conversation 2: The Virtual Father—Conversations at a Wartime Café." McSweeney's, October 2, 2009. Accessed September 20, 2016. https://www.mcsweeneys.net/articles/conversation-2-the-virtual-father.

Ravine, Jai Arun. "A Conversation Between Gabriel Ojeda-Sague and Jai Arun Ravine." *Drunken Boat Blog,* June 24, 2016. Accessed September 20, 2016. https://medium.com/drunken-boat/a-conversation-between-gabriel-ojeda-sague-and-jai-arun-ravine-fea4b9c44842#.q7xcp5v2x.

Reyes, Barbara Jane. *Diwata.* Rochester: BOA Editions Ltd., 2010.

Saijo, Albert. *Outspeaks: A Rhapsody.* Hawaii: Bamboo Ridge Press, 1997.

Samuels, Lisa. "Membranism, Wet Gaps, Archipelago Poetics." *Reading Room: A Journal of Art and Culture* 4, Liquid State special issue (2010): 156–167.

Schultz, Susan. "Susan M. Schultz on Tinfish, Interviewed by Jane Sprague." *HOW2* 2, no.4, (Spring–Summer 2006). Accessed September 20, 2016. http://www.asu.edu/pipercwcenter/how2journal/archive/online_archive/v2_4_2006/current/schultzinterview/pdfs/schultzinterview.pdf.

Tabios, Eileen. *The Thorn Rosary.* East Rockaway: Marsh Hawk Press, 2010.

Taitano, Lehua M. *A Bell Made of Stones.* Hawaii: Tinfish Press, 2013.

CONTRIBUTORS' NOTES

DON MEE CHOI is the author of *Hardly War* (Wave Books, 2016), *The Morning News Is Exciting* (Action Books, 2010), and translator of contemporary Korean women poets. She has received a Whiting Writers Award, Lannan Literary Fellowship, and Lucien Stryk Translation Prize. Her recent works also include a chapbook, *Petite Manifesto* (Vagabond Press, 2014), a pamphlet, *Freely Frayed, ㅋ=q, Race=Nation* (Wave Books, 2014), and translation of Kim Hyesoon's poetry, *Poor Love Machine* (Action Books, 2016). She was born in Seoul and came to the U.S. via Hong Kong. She now lives in Seattle.

STUART COOKE is a poet and critic based on the Gold Coast, where he lectures in creative writing and literary studies at Griffith University. His books include *Speaking the Earth's Languages: A Theory for Australian-Chilean Postcolonial Poetics* (Rodopi, 2013), *George Dyuŋgayan's Bulu Line: A West Kimberley Song Cycle* (Puncher & Wattmann, 2014), and two collections of poetry, *Opera* (Five Islands Press, 2016) and *Edge Music* (IP, 2011).

MURRAY EDMOND lives in Auckland, Aotearoa/New Zealand, and is the author of 13 poetry books and editor of three anthologies including *Big Smoke: New Zealand Poems 1960–1975,* co-edited with Alan Brunton and Michele Leggott (Auckland University Press, 2000). His book *Noh Business* (Atelos, 2005) is a study of the influence of Noh drama on the Western avant-garde. Recent publications include *Then It Was Now Again: Selected Critical Writing* (Atuanui Press, 2014); *Shaggy Magpie Songs,* poems (Auckland University Press, 2015); and *Strait Men and Other Tales,* fiction (Steele Roberts, 2015). He is the editor of the critical journal *Ka Mate Ka Ora: A New New Zealand Journal of Poetry and Poetics*, and dramaturge for Indian Ink Theatre Company.

YA-WEN HO graduated with her BA/BFA(Hons) from the University of Auckland in 2012. Her first book of long poems, *last edited [insert time here]* (Tinfish Press, 2012), documents her interest in process, found language, and cultural flotsam. In 2015, a Horoeka/Lancewood Reading Grant supported her to read for three months, at the end of which she wrote a hyper-textual essay *Dear You*. In 2016, she was the Ema Saiko Poetry Fellow in residence at the New Zealand Pacific Studio, Wairarapa. She is currently working towards an MA in Literary Translation at Victoria University of Wellington, making a case for typographic translation between Chinese and English writing systems.

MYUNG MI KIM was born in Seoul, Korea and immigrated with her family to the United States at the age of nine. Her collection of poems *Under Flag* (Kelsey) won the Multicultural Publishers Exchange Award of Merit; subsequent collections include *The Bounty* (Chax), *DURA* (Sun & Moon), *Commons* (California), *River Antes* (Atticus/Finch), and *Penury* (Omnidawn). Myung Mi Kim is the James H. McNulty Chair of English at SUNY Buffalo.

SEAN LABRADOR Y MANZANO's poem marries an unpublished poem "Hibuya," produced in K. Silem Mohammad's postLanguage course (UCSC, 2000), with the original three-page "Breaking Up with H.D.," written in a course with Miranda Mellis (Naropa, 2008), and continues themes of "The Dark Continent," written in Bharati Mukherjee's home for Stacy Doris (SFSU, 2002), which was republished in *The Best American Poetry 2004*, where attributions to Eliot, Barnes, Hemingway, and "H.D." slipped from grading undergraduate essays for Ron Loewinsohn's "American Modernists" (UCB, 2002). Presently, "H.D. in Manila," a longer work-in-progress, urged after conversing with Norma Cole, reconciles the lack of Modernist attention to literary movements in the Philippines.

SAWAKO NAKAYASU is a transnational poet and translator who has lived in Japan, France, China, and the U.S. Some of her books include *The Ants* (Les Figues Press, 2014) and *Texture Notes* (Letter Machine, 2010), and translations include *The Collected Poems of Sagawa Chika* (Canarium Books, 2015), which won the 2016 PEN Award for Poetry in Translation and The Lucien Stryk Asian Translation Prize, and Tatsumi Hijikata's *Costume en Face* (Ugly Duckling Presse, 2015). Other books include *Mouth: Eats Color—Chika Sagawa Translations, Anti-translations, & Originals*, which is a multilingual work of both original and translated poetry.

CRAIG SANTOS PEREZ is a native Chamorro from the Pacific Island of Guam. He is the author of three books, most recently *from unincorporated territory [guma']* (Omnidawn, 2014), which received an American Book Award in 2015. He is an associate professor in the English department at the University of Hawai'i, Mānoa, where he teaches Pacific Literature and Creative Writing.

MELANIE RANDS is of Hawaiian, Fijian, and Scottish descent, and is a curator, visual artist and poet based in Auckland. Committed to environmental and social change, Rands is the co-founder of ecostore, a business that makes and sells ecological products in Oceania and Asia. She co-founded an intentional community and organic farm in Matapouri Bay in Te Tai Tokelau in 1985, and is also a Greenpeace NZ board member and a member of the inaugural Pacific Advisory Group at the Auckland War Memorial Museum. Her poems have been published in *Brief #42, 2011* and *Scope: Contemporary Research Topics*, and she is currently undertaking postgraduate studies in English at the University of Auckland.

JAI ARUN RAVINE is a mixed race, mixed gender, and mixed genre artist. Their work arises from the simultaneity of text and body and takes the form of video, performance, comics, and handmade books. Ravine's first book, แล้ว *and then entwine: lesson plans, poems, knots* (Tinfish Press, 2011), re-imagines immigration history and attempts to transform cultural inheritances of silence. Their short film *Tom/Trans/Thai* approaches the silence around female-to-male (FTM) transgender identity in the Thai context and has screened internationally. Their second book, *The Romance of Siam: A Pocket Guide* (Timeless, Infinite Light, 2016) is a subverted travel guide that consumes and regurgitates orientalism, the tourist archive, and white desire. jaiarunravine.com

BARBARA JANE REYES was born in Manila, the Philippines, and grew up in the San Francisco Bay area. She earned a BA in Ethnic Studies from the University of California at Berkeley and an MFA from San Francisco State University. She is the author of the poetry collections *Gravities of Center* (Arkipelago, 2003); *Poeta en San Francisco* (Tinfish, 2005), winner of the James Laughlin Award from the Academy of American Poets; *Diwata* (BOA, 2010); and *To Love as Aswang* (Philippine American Writers and Artists, 2015).

LISA SAMUELS is a transnational poet, essayist, and sound artist who has lived in the United States, Sweden, Israel/Palestine, Yemen, Malaysia, Spain, and since 2006 in Aotearoa/New Zealand. Her works include *Tomorrowland* (Shearsman, 2009 and, as CDs, Deep Surface, 2012), *Mama Mortality Corridos* (Holloway, 2010), *Gender City* (Shearsman, 2011), *Wild Dialectics* (Shearsman, 2012), *Anti M* (Chax, 2013), *Tender Girl* (Dusie, 2015), and *Over Hear: six types of poetry experiment in Aotearoa/New Zealand* (Tinfish, 2015). She also works with composers in the U.S., New Zealand, and France and teaches literature, theory, and creative writing at The University of Auckland.

SUSAN M. SCHULTZ is author of several volumes of poetry and poetic prose, including two volumes of *Dementia Blog* (Singing Horse Press, 2008) and several volumes of *Memory Cards,* the most recent installment of which was published by Talisman House in 2016. She is author of *The Poetics of Impasse in Modern and Contemporary Poetry* from the University of Alabama Press. She wrote commentaries on Hawai'i literature for *Jacket2* and has blogged extensively on Albert Saijo's poetry and notebooks. In 2016, she won the Elliot Cades Award for Literature, which is given to writers in Hawai'i. She lives in Kāne'ohe, on the island of O'ahu, with her family.

EILEEN R. TABIOS has released about 40 collections of poetry, fiction, essays, and experimental biographies from publishers in nine countries and cyberspace. Her most recent include *Amnesia: Somebody's Memoir* (Black Radish Books, 2016) and her first bilingual edition *I Forgot Ars Poetica* translated into Romanian (Bibliotheca Universalis, 2016). Recipient of the Philippines' National Book Award for Poetry for her first poetry collection, she has also edited, co-edited, or conceptualized ten anthologies of poetry, fiction, and essays.

LEHUA M. TAITANO, a native Chamoru from Yigo, Guahån (Guam), is a queer poet, writer and artist. She is the author of *A Bell Made of Stones* (poems, Tinfish Press, 2013), a chapbook of short fiction, *appalachiapacific* (University of Montana Press, 2010), which won the 2010 Merriam-Frontier Award, and a chapbook of poetry, *Sonoma* (Drop Leaf Press, 2016). She has served as an APAture Featured Literary Artist (Kearny Street Workshop) and as a contributing Kuwentuhan poet (The Poetry Center at SFSU). Taitano currently serves as the Community Outreach Coordinator on the Executive Board of the Thinking Its Presence: Race, Literary and Interdisciplinary Studies Conference.

COREY WAKELING is the author of *Gargantuan Terrier, Buggy or Dinghy* (Vagabond Press, 2012), *Goad Omen* (Giramondo, 2013), and *The Alarming Conservatory* (Giramondo, forthcoming). With Jeremy Balius, he co-edited *Outcrop: radical Australian poetry of land* (Black Rider Press, 2013). Corey received a PhD in English and Theatre Studies from the University of Melbourne in 2013, and writes on textuality, sensation, corporeality, and experiment. He teaches literature and drama in Nishinomiya, Japan.

ACKNOWLEDGMENTS

"Freely Frayed" has been adapted from a talk for the "Translating Radical Women Poets" panel at AWP, 2014.

Portions of "Non-Local Localities: Trans-Pacific Connections Between Aboriginal and Mapuche Poetry" have been published in *Speaking the Earth's Languages: A Theory for Australian-Chilean Postcolonial Poetics* (Rodopi, 2013).

Excerpt from *Commons* (University of California Press, 2002) reprinted with permission of the author.

Excerpt from *from unincorporated territory [guma']* (Omnidawn, 2014) reprinted with permission of the author.

"The History of the Hay(na)ku" was published in *THE HAY(NA)KU ANTHOLOGY, Vol. II*, coedited by Jean Vengua and Mark Young (Meritage Press and xPress(ed), San Francisco & St. Helena and Espoo, Finland, 2008).

"White Love" and "The Romance of the Siamese Dream" are excerpts from *The Romance of Siam: A Pocket Guide* (Timeless, Infinite Light, 2016). Some versions of these pieces have previously appeared, sometimes in slightly different versions, in the following venues: "White Love" in *Streetnotes* Volume 24; "The Romance of the Siamese Dream" in *EOAGH: A Journal of the Arts* and *learning to loveDANCEmore: a performance journal* Volume 9; a section from "Under Erasure" in the *Transient* exhibition catalog.

Excerpt from *Poeta en San Francisco* (Tinfish Press, 2005) reprinted with permission of the author.

Excerpt from *Memory Cards: Albert Saijo Series* (Singing Horse Press, 2011) reprinted with permission of the author.

"i knew a boy once who was missing an eye," "national archives and records administration," "un-inc.," "a sampling from the guam visitors bureau," "below," and "my nanan biha, before death" were originally published in *Tinfish Journal* issue 20 (November 2010) and also appear in *A Bell Made of Stones* (Lehua M. Taitano, Tinfish Press, 2013).

THANKS

Warm thank yous to the Litmus Press editors and designers E. Tracy Grinnell, Emily Wang, Ashley Lamb, and HR Hegnauer; to Dagmar Vaikalafi Dyck for providing the beautiful cover art; to Rob Wilson, Elizabeth DeLoughrey, and Vicente Diaz for reading the book and contributing responses; to the University of Washington's Walter Chapin Simpson Humanities Center for Lisa's 2016 semester as a Visiting Scholar; to the University of Tokyo for a 2010 Global Studies Grant; and to the University of Auckland for co-hosting Sawako's visit to Tāmaki Makaurau / Auckland in 2010, when the idea for this book blossomed.